holy daimon

HOLY DAIMON

Frater Acher

SCARLET IMPRINT · MMXXIII

Holy Daimon, second edition
© Frater Acher 2018, 2023.
Published by Scarlet Imprint.
Illustrations by Jose Gabriel Alegría Sabogal.
Edited by Peter Grey; designed & typeset by Alkistis Dimech.

ISBN 978-1-912316-83-0 (paper)

BM BOX 77777, London WC1N 3XX · SCARLETIMPRINT.COM

CONTENTS

ILLUSTRATIONS

I do my thing and you do your thing.
I am not in this world to live up to your expectations,
And you are not in this world to live up to mine.
You are you and I am I.

And if by chance we find each other, it's beautiful,
If not, it can't be helped.

– Fritz Perls

For you are I, and I am you;
your name is mine, and mine is yours.
For I am your image.

– PGM VIII.36–38

PREFACE

Where does this doubt come from, I ask you. From weakness of faith? No! It derives logically from the unconscious awareness that too few among the priests are fiery enough to search for the path of sanctification, as do the yogis and sadhus of India. There are too few of them who take the heavenly kingdom by force. Trust me: there are more paths towards resurrection than the Church would ever dream of! The loud hoping for 'mercy' sure enough is not enough. How many of your rank are there who can say of themselves: 'As a deer pants for flowing streams, so pants my soul for you, O God'?

– Gustav Meyrink, *Der Weisse Dominikaner*

But where there is danger, there grows also what saves.

– Friedrich Hölderlin

There are three reasons why you are holding this book in your hands. While only the last one truly matters, all three shall be given here.

The World

MANY BOOKS have been written about achieving communion with our holy daimon. Unfortunately the vast majority of them have brought an exclusively magical lens to the subject. Magic, however, is worth nothing if it doesn't stand in the service of something greater. The best magic stands in the service of life. The magic of creating communion with our holy daimon is one of the most powerful forms of serving life – not only our own lives, but especially those of the many beings, large and small, visible and invisible, around us.

Even to the casual observer it could not be more obvious why such a goal would matter so critically these days. We are living in times that no longer have any appreciation of the status quo. The relative calm and peace the West experienced after the Cold War seems to be quickly fading to a distant memory. It is being pushed aside in particular by the many forces that run counter to the achievement of the UN's sustainable development goals. Among these are the following dynamics:

· A continuation of competing territorial interests over increasingly scarce natural resources and fewer remaining emerging markets.
· An institutionalized economic operating system built on a double loop of exploitation: exploitation of labour for value creation (e.g. services and goods) and exploitation of capital for financial short-term gains (e.g. dividends).
· A new wave of crusades, just like their medieval predecessors, utilizing organized religion as a means to rally the masses, create collective enemy stereotypes, and distract from pressing local issues.
· New technology and 'social' media creating the illusion of constant immediacy and ubiquitous instant gratification despite an increasing reality of individual isolation and passivity.
· A natural environment finally beginning to fight off the destructive virus called humanity which for decades has conveniently paid only lukewarm attention to its warning signs.
· And particularly in the West, a factual loss of the collective memory of the horrors of the Second World War as the first generation grows up whose grandparents did not experience those horrors firsthand. Thus nationalist agendas are on the rise again and the Pan-European social contract is at risk.

Surrounded by such disruptive and largely destructive forces, it's easy to quit caring. More than that, while these dynamics work at a global level, we still all suffer from them within our individual realities. The relentless pace of our lives, the mental numbing from the constant onslaught of images and news, the atomization of local communities, and the suffering caused by floods and storms – all these lead to a continual degradation of personal as well as collective resilience. Standing skinned and naked in life is a powerful spiritual and often necessary experience. Being left alone without support in these moments is not.

So this is the first reason why this book exists. Living a life constantly exposed to the negative forces described above, it is incredibly easy (and comfortable) to feel entitled to behave like an arse. If the world around us constantly seems to flip the bipolar switch between utter despair and aggressive exploitation, then why not do ourselves the favour of blending right in? Our holy daimon, once we have created a conscious connection with her/him, will do whatever she/he can to prevent us from making such a foolish choice. Being able to converse and commune with this powerful force, that forms the essence of who we are, replenishes us like very few other sources of resilience accessible to our species. She/he literally breathes in our pain, tiredness, and exhaustion, and breathes out the substance that rebuilds our spiritual bodies. This is no metaphor, no use of poetic language, but what communion with our holy daimon truly does for us. The reason why it sounds like romanticism is because that's how people for decades have comforted themselves and chosen to remember it – as a poetic fantasy rather than as a magical calling.

Judging without even trying is incredibly convenient – especially if it lets us remain the victims of circumstances created by global forces far beyond our realm of control or influence. Behaving like a wolf when surrounded by wolves often seems like the safest option. Unfortunately as human beings, rather than following our blood, instinct and tribe, each one of us carries the burden of first finding a vision, and then realizing a version of our noble selves.

What does it mean to be you? What does it take to live up to this meaning everyday? Nobody will be able to answer this question but you. The resources you have at your control on this journey of aspiration and exploration are limited: a finite number of days, a select group of loved ones, a fistful of dollars, and another fistful of liminal chances to prove yourself. Our holy daimon is the one exception to that rule. She/he will keep on giving if we find a way of allowing her/him to. Today our human personalities are the valves that hold back her/his force. Our holy daimon is the force that not only never runs dry, but that also knows the nameless place we keep on looking for, the place where we become who are meant to be, and fulfil our fate.

The Magic

THE SECOND REASON why this book exists is the state of decay that ritual magic has fallen into. Now, magic being in such a state is not a modern phenomenon. But what is at risk of snapping today is the chain that for centuries has been formed by direct, living lineages passed on from teachers to students. Instead of being guided by the same person for many years through many stages of magical development – a journey so individual it would never fit any grade system – what we have created today is a virtual strip mall filled with shops that sell magic as a mass-produced service on neon-lit shelves whose owners teeter on the brink of their own existence. Students have become customers, coming and going, dipping in and out of practices, quickly getting bored and treating magic like a menu to order from with the expectation of instant gratification. Such a state of decay does not affect magic itself, yet it seeps into people and generations like a poison. Rather than being a menu on a shelf, magic is a pitch black shaft that you either walk around in a wide circle or throw your entire self into. Not even Alice got to visit the white rabbit without falling for a long time first.

The idea of recreating the bond that once existed between teacher and student is certainly romantic, yet it is with equal certainty not something that the majority of twenty-first century magical students will ever experience. Only in retrospect is it that I realize my own story was a rare exception.

So this is the second reason why this book exists. Presuming we have thrown our entire selves into it, presuming we have put in several years of regular, honest, self-guided study and seen our magical skills grow, slowly, like seedlings from soil...what then?

The first years of magical apprenticeship can easily be recreated with the help of the many books and online courses available (one advantage we have over previous generations). But once we have learned to walk magically, once we have found the temple, passed through its atrium and opened the doors to the vestibule, what then? Few will make it that far. Most give up while they are still learning to lace their shoes, some get lost in the open desert, and of those remaining, many move on to founding a family just when the temple begins to come into sight. Of the small minority that keeps walking, passes through the atrium, and manages to pull open the doors of the temple, their (magical) heart is broken with a blow when they realize that the temple itself is a stage set. With the handle of the temple door still in their hand, they then look out into the same endlessly wide desert from whence they came.

Beginning to see, and then to create, our noble selves is something we each must do, by immersing ourselves entirely in our everyday reality. By making each day and each encounter matter. The same is true on a magical level. Once we move from being an apprentice to becoming an adept, our journey is no longer paved for us. It is from this moment on our magical journey that contact with our holy daimon becomes essential.

> It should never be forgotten for a single moment that the central and essential work of the Magician is the attainment of the Knowledge and Conversation of the Holy Guardian Angel. Once he has achieved this he must of course be left entirely in the hands of that Angel, who can be invariably and inevitably relied upon to lead him to the further great step – crossing of the Abyss and the attainment of the grade of Master of the Temple.[1]

When the chain that for centuries connected students to teachers breaks, the being that can take both ends and mend it is our holy daimon. Creating this chain, link by link, did not happen all at once; neither will mending it. It is a slow, generative process, watched over and perfected by each of us in partnership with our holy daimon; should we choose to do so.

---

1 Aleister Crowley, *Magic Without Tears*, 1954.

And You

THE THIRD REASON why this book exists is you, literally you, the person reading this right now. If you are reading this then you are one of a few hundred people. If you actually finish reading this book, cover to cover, then you will be one of a few dozen. Those who begin to practice its exercises will be less than can be counted on the fingers of one hand. So this is why this book exists. Because just as your holy daimon believes in you, so do I.

You matter immensely. Not in the modern sense of celebrity to which we are all encouraged to aspire, but in a much more profound way. You matter because your life sends a ripple across this planet and up into the sky. You matter because over the course of your life hundreds, thousands of spirits will be watching you, observing you, and trying to learn from you what they do not have and often do not understand: free will, ethics, kindness, and firmness, and when to use each of them. And of course, many people will watch to learn from you as well.

Most of these encounters will happen when we are not aware of them. We might be saying something, doing something that will forever leave a mark on another being, whether they are corporeal or spiritual. People and spirits will move on from us, forever changed, just as they transform us in return. That is the process by which we co-create the worlds we live in.

It would be foolish of us to aspire to be flawless in the thousands of encounters we pass through each day. Flawlessness is for tyrants and the mythical dead. As living humans, our hands are always stained. We mess up, we clean up, and mostly are blissfully ignorant of the damage or good we have done. That is not a bad state to be in. As we will explore in this book, the goal of communion with our holy daimon is not to perfect ourselves. Even our 'noble self' will still struggle and fail; it is defined not by its perfection, but by its persistent aspiration. Despite being surrounded by constant proof of the opposite, our noble self holds fast to the ideal. This Platonic idea of who we are meant to be is at one with, and yet entirely separate from, our mortal personalities. It is waiting for us within our holy daimon.

You matter immensely, not because of who you are, but because of the possibility to act that you have been given. You can begin to reach out to your holy daimon every day. Like one hand reaching out for another. From spirit to man. From inside to outside. Closing the current that brought to life all of creation. That is how you become the mender of the chain.

> One doesn't pray with words, one prays with their hands. Whoever is praying with words is begging. One doesn't beg. The spirit knows quite well what you require. When the palms touch each other, the Left is closed by help of the Right inside man to form a chain. That is how the body is bound firmly, and through the tip of the fingers, pointing upwards, a free flame arises. – That is the secret of prayers, which is not mentioned in any script.[2]

2   Gustav Meyrink, *Der Weisse Dominikaner*, 1921.

INTRODUCTION

T HIS BOOK consists of three parts, *History*, *Memory* and *Practice*, which can be read in any order. The academic in me recommends that we first ground ourselves in an historical overview of our subject. The ritualist, on the other hand, would prefer to start with a detailed firsthand account of a ritual whose purpose is to create communion with our holy daimon. My inner pragmatist hasn't even read this introduction and just opened the book on the first page of *Practice*. Irrespective of the sequence in which you read this book, there is value in each of its parts.

The *History* section offers an overview of the ideas surrounding communion with our holy daimon in three ancient cultures: the Chaldeans, the Zoroastrians and the ancient Greeks. Grounding ourselves in their concepts and ideas will greatly benefit the modern reader, for the following reasons:

· Amongst modern magicians the practice of creating communion with our holy daimon is often narrowed down to the techniques of *The Book of Abramelin* and Aleister Crowley's *Liber Samekh*. Whilst these sources have incredible value, limiting the subject to these texts significantly compromises our understanding.
· By looking at three specific and very different ancient cultures, we begin to realize how diverse, colourful, and often contradictory are the various ideas and concepts surrounding the topos of the personal daimon. Each of these cultures would have claimed orthodoxy for their spiritual ideas as well as orthopraxy for their related rites (two terms we will explore in the *Practice* section). Yet from our historical viewpoint all three cultures peacefully co-exist in the ancient past of our tradition. Understanding

the richness of our past helps us embrace the fact that there is never only one truth.

· Finally, exploring three cultures through the lens of our particular study should make it easier for you to explore further cultures on your own. In particular the Jewish mystical tradition has rich material and many advanced studies to offer. Initial leads for further exploration are the term *zelem*, as it refers to the higher image of man, and the *memuneh*, which refers to man's deputy angel.

The *Memory* section offers a complete account of my own communion with the holy daimon. Deciding to include such very personal material in this book was the second hardest choice I had to make on this journey. What finally convinced me was not its practical value to other magicians, but rather its character as a magical artefact in itself. I am offering it here as another small link in the chain and an example that this chain remains accessible to everyone. Nothing described in this book is out of reach; all that is needed is sufficient grit, persistence, and playfulness. Finally, I decided to include this personal material because of its differences from the practical path I suggest for you. Seeing these two chapters side by side – my personal journey looking backwards and your journey looking forward – should demonstrate that there is no one right way. For each of us, there is our own particular way.

The *Practice* section is what inspired this book. In late 2010 I published an essay online called 'The Everyday Path to Your Holy Guardian Angel.'[1] In it I offered a sequence of practical steps to establish communion with the holy daimon. What struck me at the time was how little 'magic' was required to achieve and maintain the goal of communion, but how much hard work was required in our mundane lives. It also struck me that acknowledging this was an oversight in most related books on the subject.

Almost ten years later – years filled with continuous, daily practice with my holy daimon – I realized that my experience on this path had progressed further, and I now saw my essay with the benefit of hindsight. While I had been right to address the importance of integrating one's

1 theomagica.com, 2010.

2

magical practice into everyday activities, I had missed an essential part of this spiritual journey; the mystical side of this spiritual path.

So in 2017 I began extended sessions of inspired writing in communion with my holy daimon. To avoid bringing through another version of the work that remained limited by my personality, I asked my daimon to take charge and to write these chapters together with me. She/he did not hesitate, but gave one condition: I was not to interfere with her/his guidance, but had to follow wherever she/he needed to take it. The sudden image that she/he gave me was the flight of an arrow, swift and straight, reaching its target.

Accepting this condition was the hardest part of writing this book. I was especially hesitant about including the last phase of the practical work, *Encounter*. There are things we get to write about, and there are things we have to explore on our own. Yet, my holy daimon was determined. She/he showed me the related sections of the Greek magical papyri she/he wanted included, told me how to make them work as a ritual, and told me to get to work. This is the result.

A final word of warning. I do not know the true nature of the being with whom I have been working every day since that night in 2010. To me she/he is my holy daimon. But does she/he have a name? Does she/he have a gender? Is she/he truly a being in his/her own right? Or maybe she/he is a spiritual gateway that I have created myself? I have no definitive answers to these questions. If magic is the bastard child of art and science, then mysticism is a bastard born of devotion and diligence. What I do know about the being whom I have come to know as my holy daimon are its effects on me, my life, and how I touch the world around me. By far her/his presence has been the greatest gift I have ever received. No other source of life, no other source of healing and happiness, compares to her/him. It is with an awareness of my ignorance that I place this book in your hands.

LVX,

Frater Acher 2018
May the serpent bite its tail.

✱

It is impossible to lay down precise rules by which a man may attain
to the knowledge and conversation of His Holy Guardian Angel; for
that is the particular secret of each one of us; a secret not to be told or
even divined by any other, whatever his grade. It is the Holy of Holies,
whereof each man is his own High Priest, and none knoweth the Name
of his brother's God, or the Rite that invokes Him.

– Aleister Crowley, One Star in Sight, *Book* 4.

PART I

HISTORY

AMONG THE CHALDEANS

Evil fiends and demons that lie in wait...Pursuing after a man, turned him from his purpose.

– Horne, 181.

SOME OF THE EARLIEST ATTESTATIONS of ritual magic date to the Chaldean period of Mesopotamian history. However, defining what the term 'Chaldean' means has long been a problem for scholars. The main challenge is that the meaning of the term has shifted repeatedly over the centuries. Originally it referred to an ancient Semitic people who first came to prominence in the late eighth century BCE, and who came to rule Babylon in 620 BCE. It is interesting to note that the Chaldeans were the culture who created the magical foundations from which many later cultures drew their astrological and ritual practices – for example the famous Sabians of Harran. Yet, the name Chaldean ceased to refer to a specific ethnic group in 539 BCE, when the Babylonian empire was absorbed into the Persian empire. Subsequently the term applies much more generally to people versed in occult teachings, particularly astrology and spells involving the planetary spirits.

It is important to remember the ambiguity of the term Chaldean as we investigate the idea of an individual spirit guardian among the 'Chaldeans.' We must also remember how few written records have come down to us from this ancient period, and that Chaldean cosmology, magical practices, and rites were all influenced by cultures which both preceded and paralleled theirs, such as the Sumerians, Assyrians and Egyptians.

Chaldean Demonology

The gods of the Euphrates, like those of the Nile, constituted a countless multitude of visible and invisible beings, distributed into tribes and
empires throughout all the regions of the universe. A particular function or occupation formed, so to speak, the principality of each one,
in which he worked with an indefatigable zeal, under the orders of his
respective prince or king; but, whereas in Egypt they were on the whole
friendly to man, or at the best indifferent in regard to him, in Chaldea
they for the most part pursued him with an implacable hatred, and only
seemed to exist in order to destroy him.

– Gaston Maspero, Vol.3, 136–137.

F OR THE CHALDEANS, daimonic forces were abundant and so were
the means to regulate human interaction with them. Man had no
real chance of confronting and surviving the constant demonic onslaught which underlay his daily life without some sort of omniscient
help. Some of these demons were even audacious enough to attack the
gods of light themselves, such as the seven wicked *maśkim*, evil subterranean demons who were counterforces to the seven planetary spirits.[1] Luckily
for man, there were good spirits who could protect him from the evil
spirits who assailed him, good spirits who existed in a dynamic dualistic
relationship with their evil counterparts – a balance comparable in its
purity only to Zoroastrianism.[2]

However, a major difference between the Zoroastrian and Chaldean
dualism is that for the Chaldeans, the continual battle between the
hordes of evil and benevolent demonic spirits was not synthesized, on the
cosmic level, into two antagonistic supreme beings. As we shall see later,
the Zoroastrians viewed Ahura Mazda, the good creator, and his antago-
nist, Ahriman, his evil adversary, as two eternally struggling forces which
formed the mythical blueprint for every struggle between the forces of
good and evil in the lower realms of creation. Chaldean cosmology, how-

1 Lenormant, 18; Butler, 5–6; Horne, 230.
2 Lenormant, 145.

ever, was much more polytheistic in tone, with divine beings residing in and bringing to life all natural phenomena.

Nevertheless, scholars have long debated whether there was some level of divine unity and successive emanation lurking beneath the surface of the apparently polytheistic Chaldean rites and incantations. One scholar who believed he could perceive such a divine unity was Lenormant:

> Underneath the exterior garb of a coarse polytheism (...) were the conceptions of a higher order from which it had originated; and foremost among them the fundamental idea of a divine unity, although disfigured by the monstrous illusions of pantheism, which confounded the creature with the Creator, and transformed the Divine Being into a multitude of derivate gods who were manifested in all the phenomena of nature.[3]

Today most scholars disagree with Lenormant's view, and consider the Chaldean religion to be polytheistic at heart. In fact, even many of his contemporary peers disagreed with him, including the respected Egyptologist Gaston Maspero:

> If the idea of uniting all these divine beings into a single supreme one, who would combine within himself all their elements and the whole of their powers, ever for a moment crossed the mind of some Chaldean theologian, it never spread to the people as a whole.[4]

If there was a supreme being from which the other gods had been born – such as the god Ilu – then it never became the centre of a cult or fellowship among the Chaldeans.[5] What has never been in doubt is that the practical aspects of Chaldean cosmology – their rites and magic – are best described as an overflowing 'adoration of the elementary spirits.'[6]

---

3 Lenormant, 111–112.
4 Maspero, Vol.3, 154.
5 Lenormant, 113–114.
6 Lenormant, 143.

The focus of the Chaldeans' religious rites were the many demonic and divine forces which they saw represented in nature and the celestial night sky: adoring the planets and their divine spirits, and obtaining their protection from their evil subterranean counterparts.[7]

> There can be no doubt of the Sabaeanism of the Chaldees, and apparently of the early Assyrians, whose pantheon, from its fusion of human and animal forms, resembles the Egyptian and Hindu. The relation of religion with astronomy is, however, more striking in Assyria than in Egypt; the system of the latter country being solar, while the Assyrian worship was rather astral. On the Babylonian cylinders and monuments, the sun and moon constantly occur, and often seven stars arranged more in the manner of the Pleiades than of the Great Bear, but probably the latter. Zodiacal signs are frequently placed in the area along with the sun, moon, and seven stars, and show unequivocally that the Greek derived their notions and arrangements of the Zodiac from the Chaldees.[8]

Magical devotions to the planetary spirits were the cornerstone of Chaldean rites; yet despite all of man's efforts to engage with them, predict their actions, and control their influence, he always remained confined by his own nature, and he continuously sought magical empowerment through divine or demonic assistance. The possibility of the direct ascension of man, of his becoming a godlike being in his own right, was never part of the Chaldean worldview. Just as they didn't strive to synthesize the plethora of gods into a single higher divine being, so they didn't strive to free man from the confines of his essential nature as a being caught in an eternal struggle between chthonic and celestial forces. The goal of Chaldean magic was to win the battle one day at a time, not to transcend it altogether.

For the Chaldean magicians, man was permanently bound into the natural realm; he had no chance of breaking free from the daimonic dual-

7 Lenormant, 112.
8 Layard, Vol.2, 440.

ism of his surroundings. Only later were ideas of theurgy and apotheosis introduced into magic – ideas of the ascension of man towards the divine and the self-directed sublimation of his nature so that he would be able to receive the governance and direction of certain spiritual realms.[9]

Upon this dualistic conception rested the whole edifice of sacred magic, of magic regarded as a holy and legitimate intercourse established by rites of divine origin, between man and the supernatural beings surrounding him. Placed unhappily in the midst of this perpetual struggle between the good and the bad spirits man felt himself attacked by them at every moment; his fate depended upon them. All his happiness was the work of the former, all the evils to which he was subject were attributable to the latter.[10]

9 Lenormant, 74, 107.
10 Lenormant, 146.

Understanding the belief system of the Chaldeans is essential if we are to grasp their perspective as it applies to a personal spirit guardian assigned to each human being. However, before we examine them, we should take a closer look at how Chaldeans understood the daimonic nature itself.

In the Jewish, Gnostic, Christian, Muslim and Neoplatonist cosmologies, the universe is arranged in a strict hierarchy, with each part having a particular place in relation to its creator. The various ranks of angels are defined by their closeness to God's throne, while the demons are in ranks which descend into increasing darkness, away from God's eternal light. The Neoplatonist chains of emanation are the purest example of this kind of cosmological ordering: they stretch out from the eternal source of creation into the abundant diversity of the material realm, creating order and alignment in what would otherwise be chaos. But, in all of these cosmologies, the organization of the universe depends ultimately on its creator. The true identity of each object and being, as well as its function in creation, rests on its relationship to the creator. But this ordering principle, so familiar to us today, is not to be found in early polytheistic cultures: it cannot be traced back to the early pantheons of the ancient Egyptians, Greeks, or Chaldeans. While polytheist religions do develop, protect, and pass on myths to do with divine creation and succession, these stories tend to carry little meaning or emphasis in daily cult practices.

Though the Chaldeans did have distinct divine hierarchies, stories about the creation of the sky and earth out of chaos, and of the overthrow of gods by their own offspring, these are of little importance and value in the rites they actually practised, rites which often centred round local gods. What mattered most to the Chaldeans was the personal relationship they developed with a particular god, spirit or demon, not how it had originally come into being. The Chaldeans viewed their gods as just as time-bound as humans: Generation after generation of divine beings handed over their devotees once their time had passed and the stars of their offspring were rising. Affairs in the spiritual realm were as fluid and unstable as in the material. As above, so below. So while Chaldean gods and demons couldn't hope for the eternal stability of their rule, they at least did not have to worry about being dependent on a single supreme being of the sort so common in later monotheistic religions.

Personal Spirit Relations

ACCORDING TO the Chaldeans, each spirit exists in its own right. Furthermore, in their animistic worldview a distinct spirit existed for every element of creation. Every plant, stone, and mineral; every animal or artefact created by humans; everything that existed came with a spirit attached. Nothing was organized in the sort of sympathetic chains that we find in the later Hellenistic period.[11]

What mattered to the Chaldean mage wasn't discovering where gods or demons came from, but striking positive alliances with the benevolent ones and aiming deadly blows at the wicked ones. He was concerned with the personal impact that each spirit could have on him, not their genealogy. A Chaldean mage did not worry about ascending into the heavens through theurgy. Spiritual actions were valued for their immediate effect, with no thought of recreating any bond with a distant primordial creator god. To borrow a kabbalistic expression, for the Chaldeans Kether always rested solidly in Malkuth.

This is why there was no notion among the Chaldeans of a transcendent or supralunar personal daimon assigned to each human at birth. Chaldeans would have frowned at Crowley's maxim, 'Every man and woman is a star.' They did not think of humans (or their higher selves) as stars in their own right: magically, their focus was on binding the spirits of specific stars to humans or sacred objects.[12] Indeed, for Chaldean magic to work at all, the difference between the human realm and the realm of the stars was essential. The stars, who were messengers from and to the divine realm,[13] had to be invoked into the human realm precisely because they were alien to it.

> Stars function in a dual role in relation to man: they exert a direct influence and serve as mediators between man and god. Directly, through astral irradiation, they transform ordinary substances into potent ones that will be effective in magic, medicine, or ritual, as Materia Medica,

11 Reiner, 141.
12 Reiner, 127–128, 139.
13 Reiner, 16.

amulets, or cultic appurtenances. Stars also provide reliable answers to the query of the diviner. More important, in their second role stars are man's medium of communication with the divine.[14]

For the deeply pragmatic Chaldean mage, the point of his magic was to create whatever spirit bonds were most appropriate for a given situation; not to achieve a single transcendent union of spirit which was owed to him as a birthright. Good luck, health, wealth, and longevity were what he was after; and these things were to be got through deliberately chosen magical patrons, spirit alliances and demon traps, not through some higher state of being that could be unlocked only through mystical ascension.

Though the Chaldeans had no time for the idea of a supracelestial holy daimon, there are many examples of individual spirits acting as familiars or patrons to humans for both good and evil ends;[15] spirit alliances were crucial to the Chaldeans for their survival. And demonic possession – the most intimate type of spirit communion – was not only possible, but common. Though such possession was naturally dreaded when the possessing demon was evil, and treated with exorcism, it could equally be intentionally induced when the demon in question was viewed as useful.

Here is an example of an incantation to protect from possession by an evil spirit:

> The wicked god, the wicked demon, the demon of the desert, the demon of the mountain, the demon of the sea, the demon of the marsh, the evil genius, the enormous *uruku*, the bad wind itself, the wicked demon which seizes the body, which disturbs the body. Spirit of the heavens, conjure it! Spirit of the earth, conjure it![16]

And here is an example of an incantation to induce beneficial possession:

> The king, the shepherd of his people, may he (hold) the sun in his right hand, may he (hold) the moon in his left hand. May the favourable

14 Reiner, 15.
15 Reiner, 109.
16 Lenormant, 3.

demon, the favourable giant, which governs the lordship and the crown, penetrate into his body![17]

However, demonic influence, whether good or evil, was always perceived as an entirely external intervention in the human realm. Demonic influence was always an outside influence. No demon was naturally connected to man's soul. As a denizen of an animist world filled with influencing spirits, it was man's everyday interaction with these beings that brought about afflictions, ill fate, and various forms of diseases (and equally boons, good luck, and rude health):

> They, the products of the infernal regions, on high they bring trouble, and below they bring confusion. Falling in rain from the sky, issuing from the earth, they penetrate the strong timbers, the thick timbers; they pass from house to house. Doors do not stop them, bolts do not stop them, they glide in at the doors like serpents, they enter by the windows like the wind.[18]

While the idea of an inborn holy daimon didn't exist for the Chaldeans, the later Babylonian sorcerers deliberately created bonds with demonic patrons, which were bound either into objects or directly into human beings.

Here is an example of an incantation to the guardian spirit of king Esarhaddon, a king of Assyria who reigned between 681 and 669 BCE:

> May the guardian bull, the guardian genius, who protects the strength of my throne, always preserve my name in joy and honour until these feet move themselves from their place.[19]

---

17 Lenormant, 35.
18 Lenormant, 30.
19 Lenormant, 54.

Summary

HE CHALDEANS, one of the earliest cultures to influence our Western magical tradition, did not have the concept of a personal holy daimon of the sort known in later centuries. However, one potential source of the idea of the holy daimon is their use of demonic patrons or guardian spirits. This was an established practice in their magic, and an important method for warding and gaining protection from evil influences. Furthermore, the idea of individual mystical or magical ascension was unknown to them. In a world where spiritual genealogy meant little and efficacious curses and protection charms meant everything, man's goal was not to spiritualize himself or to escape the physical boundaries of his existence. Rather than aspiring to reconnect with his personal star, the Chaldean mage worked to connect with those stars most helpful in resolving whatever problem was at hand.

✳   ✳

✳

AMONG THE ZOROASTRIANS

Although the Greater Bundahishn or Creation was written in Middle Persia in the ninth century BCE, this work preserves older traditions about the teachings of Zarathustra or Zoroaster, a religious reformer on the steppes of southern Russia late in the second millennium. Challenging the prevailing polytheism, his creed entered eastern Iran about 1200 and moved west to the Iranian tribes of Media by about 600.

– Brian P. Copenhaver

A N ANCIENT TRADITION like Zoroastrianism is a strong tree with many branches and deep taproots. Trying to identify a single line of tradition or ritual practice would not only be naive, but would neglect the beauty that such a rich tradition has to offer. As a result, this chapter features many lengthy quotes. Primary and secondary sources on Zoroastrianism are vast, and still relatively unknown among Western magicians. As a result the reader may find some of this chapter's conclusions surprising but they will be backed by academic testimony.

Understanding the origins of the concept of the holy daimon is impossible without understanding the significant influence of Zoroastrianism. Just as Zoroastrianism influenced the later monotheistic religions,[1] its ideas about personal spirit guardians profoundly influenced the Western occult tradition.

---

1 Moore, 181; Scheftelowitz, Vorwort.

Zoroastrianism had its origin in a branch of the great Iranian race. It rose to power as the religion of the Medo-Persian empire, and while it spread widely among the subject peoples, particularly in Asia Minor, its strongholds were always the Iranian lands (...).[2]

As soon as we try to date the origins of Zoroastrianism as we might date the origins of the various religious beliefs of the ancient Hindus, Egyptians and Chaldeans – and indeed the later monotheistic religions such as Judaism and Christianity – then we find ourselves faced with a fundamental problem: the origin of Zoroastrianism in ancient Persia has yet to be firmly established. Surprisingly, we find vast variations of more than two thousand years in scholarly estimates of the religion's genesis: different experts have located this anywhere from 3000 to 600 BCE. This is due to the fact that despite its antiquity, Zoroastrianism only enters recorded history in the middle of the fifth century BCE.[3] Even then, the earliest attestation of Zoroaster's existence, which places him in the sixth century BCE, seems to be flawed:

> By now it is agreed by almost all scholars actively working in the field that this date is in fact fictitious, calculated piously but quite erroneously by Persian Magi, perhaps early in the Christian era, in order to place Zoroaster in a historical setting and so make him equal in this respect with Jesus and the Gnostic prophets of that time.[4]

It appears that the dispute about the real age and origin of Zoroastrianism has a long history which stretches all the way back to the Magi of antiquity and the Greek philosophers.[5] But irrespective of Zoroastrianism's exact date of origin, we do know a lot about the religion's content and cosmology. Probably the most important source are the Gathas, a compendium of loosely connected ancient hymns that are said to have been composed by Zoroaster himself.

2 Moore, 181.
3 Kingsley, 245.
4 Boyce, quoted in Kingsley, 245.
5 Kingsley, 245.

From these early sources we learn that the most distinct aspect of creation is the eternal struggle between two opposing forces, and this is played out on various levels of existence. On the divine level we find the concepts of *ahuras* and *daevas*.[6] First and foremost among the *ahuras* is Ahura Mazda or Spenta Mainyu,[7] the principal creator god and the only *ahura* mentioned by name in the Gathas.[8] The eternal struggle between Ahura Mazda, and his devil-opponent, Ahriman or Angra Mainyu,[9] is the foundation and background of every earthly event and fate, and the central divine dynamic within Zoroastrianism.[10]

Life is co-operation with good and conflict with evil. Good and evil are co-existing polarities. Man can think of things only in terms of their opposites. Light is light because of darkness. Health is a coveted boon, as its loss heralds sickness. Life is valued as Ahura Mazda's most incomparable gift, as lurking death threatens its extinction. Happiness is pleasant, for misery is unbearable. Riches rise in worth owing to the dread of poverty. Joy is gratifying, for sorrow aims at killing it. Virtue is the health of the spirit, for vice is its disease. Righteousness is the life of the spirit, for wickedness spells its death. There can be no compromise between good and evil. Incessant warfare is raging between good and evil. Man's duty is to commend good and co-operate with it; to condemn evil and enter into conflict with it.[11]

Man is given an active role to play in this transcendent battle. He is put in the middle of two opposing forces: on the one side truth and order, and on the other chaos, falsehood and destruction. Thanks to his free will, he has an active choice to support either the forces of Ahura Mazda

6 Blois, 3. The latter term survives in modern Persian as *dew*, Western Persian *div*, 'demon.'

7 'Holy Spirit,' ref. Dhalla (1914), 48.

8 Note, this is why Zoroastrianism is also called Mazdaism, according to the principle divine being's name being Ahura Mazda.

9 i.e. 'Evil Spirit,' ref. Dhalla (1914), 48.

10 Panati, 252, 358.

11 Dhalla (1938), chapter X.

or Ahriman; and this will tip the scales and ultimately decide the fate of life and all creation. The importance of leading an ethical life is deeply embedded in Zoroastrian religion. Pursuing truth and order through good thoughts, good words, and good deeds was central to its everyday practice. Furthermore, man's relationship with the divine is less that of a subordinate and more that of a devoted partner or a co-creator of reality.

The eternal battle between Ahura Mazda and Ahriman occurs at the most transcendent layer of creation, where these two opposing forces collide. Yet, as we will see later, on the next, lower layer – the layer closely connected with the nature of the human soul – this struggle is fought just as hard.[12] And it is here that we shall encounter one of the earliest recorded versions of the concept of the holy daimon. Before that, however, it will be helpful to take a brief look at the fundamental beliefs of Mazdean demonology.

✳

12 Blois, 4.

Mazdean Demonology

In the ninth-century Pahlavi books, dualism is omnipresent. Good and
evil forces are presented in an almost perfect symmetry, and for each
good creature a symmetrical evil corresponds.

– Moazami, 301.

CCORDING TO the dualistic Mazdean cosmology, the primordial
evil being Ahriman or Angra Mainyu ('destructive spirit') is the
creator of all that is evil, destructive, and chaotic. Assigning all evil
creations directly to him solved many complex theological problems
for Zoroastrianism,[13] as they didn't have to explain why a genuinely
positive creator god would have created evil. Most Zoroastrian sources,
such as the Vendīdād or the Bundahishn, simply say that it was Ahriman
himself who brought forth all chaos, evil, sicknesses, and – first and foremost – the evil demons called *daevas*.

The infernal crew. The diabolic spirits who have entered into a compact
with Angra Mainyu to mar the good creation of Ahura Mazda are the
Daevas, or demons. They are the offspring of the Evil Mind and spread
their mischief over all the seven zones. The Evil Spirit has taught them
to mislead man through evil thought, evil word, and evil deed.[14]

Apart from Ahriman himself, the source texts mention six, or more rarely
seven, main *daevas*. Beyond this inner circle of evil spirits, vast hordes of
additional and increasingly lowly evil spirits spread out into the material
realm. Their numbers extend into infinity, as new demons are constantly
brought to life by the evil deeds of every creature:

Various new *devs* are those who spring on to the creatures, ever and
anon, out of the sins which they commit.[15]

13 Russel, 73.
14 Dhalla (1914), 49.
15 Bundahishn XXVII.51.

The source of all these evil demons is Ahriman's relentless desire to counter the benign creation of Ahura Mazda. This motive is clear in the creation account of the main six *daevas*, each of whom is the antithesis of one of the six Amesha Spentas (see table), the divine sparks of Ahura Mazda.

DAEVA (EVIL DEMON)	MEANING	AMESHA SPENTA (DIVINE SPARK)	MEANING	RULERSHIP
Akoman	'evil thought'	Vohu Manah	'good purpose'	Animals
Indar	'who freezes the mind'	Asha Vahishta	'righteousness'	Fire
Sarvar	'oppression'	Kshatra Vairya	'desirable dominion'	Metals & minerals
Nanghait	'discontent'	Spenta Armaiti	'holy devotion'	Earth
Tawrich	'destruction'	Haurvatat	'wholeness'	Water
Zariz	'who poisons plants'	Ameretat	'immortality'	Plants

As Ahura Mazda holds his council of celestial beings, so Angra Mainyu maintains in his infernal court a retinue of male and female demons. In opposition to every archangel and angel (...) the younger literature sets up a corresponding fiend. These form exact counterparts of the powers of goodness, and always act in direct opposition to them. We do not find the symmetry of diametric opposites between these rival forces carried out to completion in the extant Gathic literature. The names of not all the corresponding demons, who are the opponents of Mazda's ministering angels, are found.[16]

The basic antagonism between the six highest Zoroastrian angels and demons mirrors the war between the two eternal divine principles Ahura Mazda and Ahriman, but on a lower cosmological level. It is this principle of antagonistic demonic and angelic forces that we rediscover in the Solomonic tradition several centuries later.

16 Dhalla (1914), 49.

The Solomonic Connection

OR PRACTITIONERS of the traditional ritual magic of the West, the correspondence between the seventy-two spirits of the Ars Goetia and the seventy-two angels of the Shem HaMephorash is the most famous example of dualism between angelic and demonic forces wherein each power is balanced by the power of its opponent. A fascinating development of this can be found in the seventeenth century grimoire of Dr Thomas Rudd, who matched the seals of the goetic demons with corresponding angelic seals.[17] A full account of all seventy-two antagonisms can be found in Carroll Runyon's *The Book of Solomon's Magick* (consolidated in the 'Master Mandala') and in Stephen Skinner and David Rankine's *The Goetia of Dr Rudd*.

Adam McLean, in his *A Treatise on Angel Magic*, characterizes the dualism present in Rudd's works in a simplistic fashion, viewing it as nothing more than an expression of a 'primitive dualism,'[18] which he explains as an unfortunate legacy of the 'Jewish patriarchal religion.'[19] According to McLean, this dualism is evidence of our ancestors' inability to understand evil as 'nothing else but an encounter of the magician with his unconscious mind.'[20] According to McLean, encountering evil in the outside world is a projection that 'must be integrated in order to avoid pathological conditions arising through repressing in a dualistic way a side of our being.'[21] Without passing judgement on what appears to be a highly Eurocentric take on ritual magic, and demonic evocation in particular, McLean's identification of Jewish influence as the root cause for this historic dualism is at the very least shortsighted. His claim that 'before this period magicians could work naturally to invoke spirits without any inner qualms'[22] is questionable: this certainly was not the case in many pre-Christian cultures. As we have seen in the previous chapter, some

17 Skinner *&* Rankine, 73.
18 McLean, 15.
19 McLean, 13.
20 McLean, 14.
21 McLean, 13.
22 McLean, 13.

ancient cultures did indeed divide the spiritual realm into benevolent and malefic beings and prohibited any evocation of the latter sort; this was equally true of Zoroastrian magic.[23]

Both the title of 'Magi' for the devotees of Zoroastrianism, and Pliny the Elder's comment that Zoroaster was the inventor of magic, are misleading. Sorcery is condemned in the harshest way in every Zoroastrian text that mentions it. Zoroaster himself labelled magicians as the hands, feet, eyes and ears of the evil spirit Ahriman.[24] Though the mythical Zoroaster was held in high regard as a master of astrology, his connection with magic was introduced much later, and deliberately, by the Greeks.[25]

Rather than being essentially magical, most Zoroastrian religious rituals were exacting cleansing and purification rites. To understand the development of these rites, we first need to take a closer look at the Zoroastrian view of the nature of matter.

The Nature of Matter

In Zoroastrian literature, the Evil Spirit's creation has a negative character because it begins in opposition to that of the Beneficent Spirit. The material state is the creation of the Beneficent Spirit; the Evil Spirit can only attack, contaminate, and corrupt it.

– Mahnaz Moazami, 316.

ACCORDING TO ZOROASTRIANISM, the world had already been fully created when the first evil spiritual beings came into existence. Before the *daevas* arrived, all creation was in perfect harmony: the idea of either a human or divine Fall, as found in Lurianic Kabbalah for example, is not found in Zoroastrianism. Only upon the arrival of the *daevas*, and as a result of their actions, did evil start to exist and actively affect humans – and indeed the whole material realm. According to Zoroastrianism, matter itself has a perfect and pure nature, and demons

23 Kiesewetter, 123.
24 Kiesewetter, 123.
25 Beck, 2002.

can affect the life forces encapsulated in the world of creation only by penetrating through matter. According to Mazdean cosmology, every evil demonic being depends on matter to materialize itself on any level of creation. Thus the nature of demons is essentially parasitic, as they require a foreign body or shell to dwell in. Their primal and most deeply rooted urge is to enter the world of substance to be clothed in matter and become effective beings in the physical realm.[26]

Once a demon has managed to break into a body, they can exert a direct influence on the spirit residing in it. Then, in accordance with their own nature, they change the feelings, behaviour, and thoughts of the spirit whose body they have entered, and trigger a process of moral and physical corruption that ultimately leads to decay.

For Zoroastrians, demonic influence was not restricted to humans: it was also to be found in the animal, plant, metal and mineral kingdoms. In the animal realm demonic influence was particularly clear, they categorized each animal as either beneficial or maleficent. Such a division is especially important when we consider that animals were considered to be intermediaries between humanity and the divine or demonic worlds.[27]

✳

26 ref. Bruce Lincoln during a lecture at Duke University in 2010.
27 Moazami, 317.

The Demonic Animal

The animal world is likewise divided between 'beneficial' animals, creatures of the Beneficent Spirit, and 'maleficent' animals, creatures of the Evil Spirit. The partition of animals as beneficial or maleficent represents one of the most important and original aspects of the ancient Iranian religious worldview.[28]

WHILE THE PHYSICAL BODIES of animals were originally created by Ahura Mazda, many of their spirits were later overtaken by the sinfulness and malevolence of Ahriman. These maleficent animals, called *xrafstars*, corrupted Ahura Mazda's benign creation and become agents of the Evil Spirit. Their influence was directed not only against the benevolent creatures, but also against the raw elements of creation itself: water, fire, earth, and plant life. Evil animals functioned as parasitic forces of pollution, impurity, and destruction from within creation itself.[29]

The Bundahishn (…) divides evil animals by whether they live in the water, on earth, or in the air – of the water, the frog; of the earth, the many-headed dragon; and of the air, the winged snake are the worst.[30]

The killing of evil animals was an important form of devotion among the Magi. Not only was this done collectively on important dates in their ritual calendar to honour the feminine angelic spirit of earth, Spandarmad, but it was also practised individually as a way to atone for grave sins. Given that the long lists of evil animals assigned to the night included most species of snakes, reptiles, amphibians, and flying and crawling insects, we may rightly wonder whether an echo of the idea of the demonic animal is to be found in the convoluted recipes attributed to the medieval witches; especially as Zoroastrian sources state that the bodies of dead evil animals may be used to prepare remedies. This was possible because the

28 Moazami, 301.
29 Moazami, 301, 302.
30 Moazami, 302.

malevolent spirit was cut off from its animal host once the physical body was dead, leaving only the pure physical remains, made of the benevolent elements of water, earth, wind and fire.[31]

Another striking similarity between the Zoroastrian rosters of evil animals and the iconography of the medieval witch is the cat, which in both cases was viewed as an evil animal associated particularly with demons and sorcerers. Considering that ancient Iranians were nomads, perhaps they would have considered cats ambiguous, restive, and perfidious, quite unlike the loyal dogs that watched over their cattle and tents.[32]

From the above, two central characteristics of the Zoroastrian cult become obvious: First, its deeply entrenched dualism leaves no space for any shades of grey. It was impossible to contact any spiritual being through prayer whose nature wasn't clearly delineated as either good or evil. The demarcation line between good and evil even extended into the land of the fairies. A person's ritual actions, just as much as their everyday decisions, testified as to whether they were ultimately on the side of the forces of good or evil. And second, the main corpus of the Zoroastrian cult was aimed at the cleansing and purification of substance and matter. After all, an eternal divine battle was being fought over immanence in matter itself, i.e. whether creation would maintain its inborn purity and benevolence thanks to the guardianship of watchful angelic beings, or lose it through the malice, cunning, and destructiveness of evil spirits.[33]

A class of bewitching fairies has been created by Angra Mainyu to seduce men from the right path and injure the living world. Nimble as birds they go along flying in the shape of shooting stars between the earth and the heavens. They come upon fire, water, trees, and other creations from which they are to be driven away by the recital of spells.[34]

---

31 Moazami, 308.

32 Moazami, 314.

33 Russell, 76; Kiesewetter, 120, 134.

34 Dhalla (1914), 172.

The Constitution of Man

I N OUR DISCUSSION of the main aspects of Mazdean demonology, we learned that man had a crucial role to play in ending the onslaught of evil and helping the forces of Ahura Mazda to overcome the eternal fiend. The struggle between good and evil took place on all levels of creation, encompassing the divine, demonic, angelic, and human worlds. Thus, unsurprisingly, we find that every man possessed two demons bound into his own nature: an evil demon and an beneficial angel. The Zoroastrian texts call these beings 'twins,'[35] the 'animal' and 'angel' within man, or simply the lower and the higher selves. While the higher self supports the evolution of man towards light and righteousness, the animal within him is constantly laying pitfalls in his way, hoping that he will stumble over desires, false needs, and deceiving emotions behind which the 'animal' lies in wait.

Man was animal but yesterday. Today he is man, though not devoid of animal traits. His destiny is to be angel, and tomorrow he shall be that also. Everyone has in his or her power to be a saint. But the way to attain sainthood and divinity is distant and beset with countless difficulties. Every step in advance is a struggle. The animal in man is obdurate and persistent, cunning and resourceful. To escape from his grip, to destroy his power, to eliminate him, man has to fight a hundred battles. Man's inner life is a perpetual warfare between animal and human within his breast. A violent struggle is going on in every human heart between the higher impulses to renounce animal appetites, and the lower instincts to satisfy them. Man is a divided self, divided mind, divided will, and feels within him the conflict of two opposing natures. The one half of man's being is always at war with his other half. When the Good Spirit first met the Evil Spirit, he said that he was opposed to him in his thoughts and words and deeds and faith and conscience and soul and every thing. The same complete polarity obtains between the higher self and the lower self in man.[36]

35 Blois, 4; Carnoy, 864.
36 Dhalla (1938), chapter X.

It is here that we perhaps encounter the first example of what became the philosophy of the 'Holy Genius and Evil Demon' as portrayed in the *Divine Pymander* of the *Corpus Hermeticum* in the second or third century CE:

> (...) for I the Mind [the *logos* or holy genius] come unto men that are Holy and good, pure and merciful, and that live piously and religiously; and my presence is a help unto them. (...) But to the foolish, and evil, and wicked, and envious, and covetous, and murderous, and profane, I am far off, giving place to the revenging Demon, which applying unto him the sharpness of fire, tormenteth such a man sensible, and armeth him the more to all wickedness, that he may obtain the greater punishment. And such an one never ceaseth, having unfulfilled desires, and unsatisfiable concupiscences, and always fighting in darkness; for the Demon always afflicts and tormenteth him continually, and increaseth the fire upon him more and more.[37]

> I myself, the mind, am present to the blessed and good and pure and merciful – to the reverent – and my presence becomes a help; (...) But from these I remain distant – the thoughtless and evil and wicked and envious and greedy and violent and irreverent – giving way to the avenging demon who [wounds the evil person], assailing him sensibly with the piercing fire and thus arming him the better for lawless deeds so that greater vengeance may befall him. Such a person does not cease longing after insatiable appetites, struggling in the darkness without satisfaction. [This] tortures him and makes the fire grow upon him all the more.[38]

Thus the notion that man is torn between the inner guidance of two opposing spiritual beings can be traced from Zoroastrianism all the way to the *Hermetica*. Moreover, evidence of this belief is visible in early Christian scriptures, such as the *Shepherd of Hermas* from the first or second century CE:

37 Westcott, 27–28.
38 *The Hermetica*, Copenhaver (1992), 5.

29

₇And now, says he; understand first of all what belongs to faith. There are two angels with man; one of righteousness, the other of iniquity. ₈And I said unto him: Sir, how shall I know that there are two such angels with man? Hear says he, and understand. ₉The angel of righteousness, is mild and modest, and gentle, and quiet. When therefore, he gets into thy heart, immediately he talks with thee of righteousness, of modesty, of chastity, of bountifulness, of forgiveness, of charity, and piety. ₁₀When all these things come into thy heart, know then that the angel of righteousness is with thee. Wherefore hearken to this angel and to his works. ₁₁Learn also the works of the angel of iniquity. He is first of all bitter, and angry, and foolish; and his works are pernicious, and overthrow the servants of God. When therefore these things come into thy heart; thou shalt know by his works, that this is the angel of iniquity.³⁹

Some thirteen centuries later, the same philosophy of man's soul is repeated in that most famous compendium of medieval Western magic, Agrippa's *Three Books of Occult Philosophy* (1531–1533):

As therefore there is given to every man a good spirit, so also there is given to every man an evil Diabolical spirit, whereof each seeks an union with our spirit, and endeavours to attract it to itself, and to be mixed with it, as wine with water; the good indeed, through all good works conformable to itself, change us into Angels, by uniting us, as it is writ of John Baptist in Malachi: behold I send mine Angel before thy face: of which transmutation, and union it is writ elsewhere; He which adheres to God is made one spirit with him. An evil spirit also by evil works, studies to make us conformable to itself, and to unite, as Christ saith of Judas, Have not I chosen twelve, & one of you is a devil? And this is that which Hermes saith, when a spirit hath influence upon the soul of man, he scatters the seed of his own notion, whence such a soul being sown with seeds, and full of fury, brings forth thence wonderful things, and whatsoever are the offices of spirits: for when a good spirit hath

39 *Shepherd of Hermas*, Command VI: 7–11, 218–219.

influence upon a Holy soul, it doth exalt it to the light of wisdom; but an evil spirit being transfused into a wicked soul, doth stir it up to theft, to manslaughter, to lusts, and whatsoever are the offices of evil spirits.[40]

ELEMENT	PURPOSE	AFTER DEATH RETURNS TO	DESCRIPTION
Baodhagh (body)	Connection to matter	Earth	Man's physical force and nature
Uštana (life)	Connection to wind and complexion	Wind	Vital principle
Urvan (soul)	Connection to the mind and senses	*Fravashi*	Conscious mind; characterizing individuality
Aghva (prototype)	Connection to the Sun	Sun	Self, the seat of life
Fravashi	Connection to Ahura Mazda	-	Supreme spiritual principle

According to Mazdean sources, man is composed of five elements (see table above). We do not know the level at which the Zoroastrians believed the fight between the lower and higher selves of man occurred. Perhaps the struggle took place at every level, or perhaps it occurred between specific elements of his constitution, such as between his *baodhagh*, the animal nature of his body, and his *aghva*, his higher self. Given that Zoroastrianism is known to have influenced the early phases of Judaism, perhaps the latter interpretation might find some support in the Jewish tradition of the good and evil urge. Both the Talmud and the Zohar know this principle, one that often keeps man trapped between good and evil, unable to fulfil his true destiny. According to the Zohar, the good inclinations spring from the highest level of the soul, the *neshamah*,[41] whereas the evil urge attaches itself to the body of a baby at its moment of birth.[42]

40 Agrippa, Book 3, chapter XX, 521–522.
41 Prophet, 167.
42 Müller, 152.

We learn from Zoroastrian scripture that it is first and foremost the *urvan*, the soul of man, that requires protection from the afflictions of evil if it is not to degenerate and decay:

> And in that wind he saw his own religion and deeds as a profligate woman, naked, decayed, gaping, bandy-legged, lean-hipped, and so spotted so that spot was joined to spot, like the most hideous, noxious creature, most filthy and most stinking. Then that wicked soul spoke thus: 'Who art thou, than whom I have never seen any creature of Auharmazd and Akharman uglier, or filthier, or more stinking?' To him she spoke thus: 'I am thy bad actions, O youth of evil thoughts, of evil words, of evil deeds, of evil religion. It is on account of thy will and actions that I am hideous and vile, iniquitous and diseased, rotten and foul-smelling, unfortunate and distressed, as it appears to thee.'[43]

Luckily, man had a strong ally at his side in his fight against the evil within and around him. According to Mazdean tradition, this is his *fravashi*, his personal defender spirit.

✶

---

43 *The Book of Arda Viraf* (226–640 CE), chapter XVII, in Müller, 205.

The Fravashi

The *fravashi*, or guardian-spirit, is a totally distinct spiritual adjunct which every individual and object of the good creation possesses; it is a kind of primary idea, and is the spiritual counterpart of a deceased person, that is invoked, or reverenced, in certain ceremonies. Its duty is to protect the body which it represents.[44]

I N THE ZOROASTRIAN worldview, the essential antidote to all demonic affliction was the *fravashi*. As soon as anything was created, it was assigned a 'double or spirit form.'[45] In the relationship between the *fravashi* and the material body that it guards, we find another proof of Zoroastrianism's positive view of matter, for having a physical body was the prerequisite of being assigned a personal spirit guardian. The *fravashis* were individual spirit patrons for everything made of matter, and embodied 'the simple essence of all things, the celestial creatures corresponding with the terrestrial, of which they were the immortal types.'[46]

For anybody familiar with Plato's theory of forms, this might sound suspiciously similar to his concept of 'ideas.' As a disciple of Socrates, Plato recorded and expanded upon his teacher's view that all material forms were connected to the realm of the essential good or divine. According to one of Plato's most famous premises, a material form had the same relationship with the divine idea from which it emerged as a shadow had with the object by which it was cast. The shadow itself is ephemeral and has no substance; rather the object that casts it has actual structure and solidity. This allegory of Plato's, which claimed that our physical reality was really nothing but the distorted reflection of an original reality populated by divine ideas, initiated one of the most significant paradigm shifts in the history of thought, as it inverted the locus of ontological reality from the physical realm to the divine realm.

Plato did not consider the material realm to be completely illusory, however: a shadow exists somewhere between an illusion of, and a

44 West, 606.
45 Horne, 2.
46 Lenormant, 199.

representation of, the object which casts it. And just as a shadow can hint at what casts it, so the material realm allows conclusions to be drawn about the shape and nature of the divine reality. The changeable material realm is caught in a process of constantly 'miming' the good or divine forms from which it emerges. And with this knowledge, man's purpose could easily be divined. Our species' proper service to the Good was its cooperation in implementing the ideal in the world of shadows; that is, in miming the Good.

The apparent affinity between Zoroastrianism and Platonism has long been recognized, and it has even been suggested that Zoroaster was the chief authority behind Plato. Whatever the truth, such musings certainly ensured the lasting popularity of Zoroaster's name among scholars, especially those writing in the fifteenth and sixteenth centuries.[47]

Returning to the subject of the *fravashis*, however, there is no evidence that they were viewed as the 'real' objects lurking behind the Platonic shadowplay. Rather, both the material being and its spiritual double were held to be real, but existed on different levels. Humans, animals, plants, and crystals were mortal creatures who dwelt in the material realm, and the *fravashis* were their immortal celestial counterparts. And while the *fravashis* indeed created the matrices of life for their respective material beings, both parties had an independent, individual existence: the latter ephemeral, the former eternal. Thus every created being was viewed as having its own fixed point or guiding principle in the shape of its individually assigned *fravashi*. The *fravashis*:

> are like the guardian-angels of all individual persons. They are a duplicate of the soul, existing before birth and uniting themselves with the soul after death. Their name seems to mean 'confession', 'conscience,' and it may be an equivalent of the daena, the 'conscience' or 'religion' which survives a man and is shaped after his conduct during life.[48]

---

47 Hanegraaff, 1183.
48 Carnoy, 865.

As far as the Zoroastrians were concerned, the idea of man having both a holy genius and an evil demon attached to his soul was not considered to be irreconcilable with the idea of his having only one immortal holy daimon.

Man was constantly tormented by his evil urge and had to battle demonic attacks from within and around him if he was to fulfil his purpose in creation and follow his good urge with 'good thoughts, good words, and good deeds.' The dualistic struggle between good and evil was not something one could ever hope to decisively resolve; rather, one's essential purpose in creation was to endure it and to tilt the balance ever further in the favour of the forces of good. Each individual had his own celestial ally in his personal *fravashi*, a safe place of powerful protection against evil, and a place of personal guidance and counsel. Therefore, we might consider the *fravashi* an early ancestor of Socrates' personal *daimonion*. As an individually-assigned 'unseen agent,'[49] in the *fravashi* we encounter, for the first time, the idea of an immortal and self-conscious higher being completely dedicated to guiding and protecting its mortal counterpart through the struggles of everyday life:

> The *fravashis*, however, are not restricted to the departed, though their fravashis are most frequently invoked. Every being, whether living or dead, has its *fravashi*, its unseen agent, which is joined to the body at the time of birth, and leaves it again at the time of death. The *fravashis* remind us of the Greek *daimones* and the Roman *genii*. The *fravashis* belong to the spiritual, the body to the material creation. Not only men, but the gods also, Ormazd, the sacred word, the sky, the water, the plants, all have their *fravashis*. We may call the *Fravashi* the genius of anything.[50]

The glory and praise that the influence and powers of the *fravashi* receive in Mazdean ritual practice is well illustrated in the following quote from the Fravardin Yasht (probably 559–330 BCE):

49 Müller, 205.
50 Müller, 205.

Ahura Mazda spoke to Spitama Zarathushtra: To thee alone I shall
tell the power and strength, glory, usefulness, and happiness of the
Holy guardian angels, the strong and victorious, O righteous Spitama
Zarathushtra! how they come to help me. By means of their splendour
and glory I uphold the sky which is shining so beautifully and which
touches and surrounds this earth; it resembles a bird which is ordered
by God to stand still there; it is high as a tree, wide-stretched, iron-bod-
ied, having its own light in the three worlds. Ahura Mazda, together
with Mithra, Rashnu, and Spenta Armaiti, puts on a garment decked
with stars and made by God in such a way that nobody can see the
ends of its parts. By means of the splendour and glory of the fravashis
I uphold the high strong Anahita (the celestial water) with bridges, the
salutary who drives away the demons, who has the true faith and is to
be worshipped in the world. If the strong guardian-angels of the righteous should not give me assistance then cattle and men, the two last of
the hundred classes of beings, would no longer exist for me; then would
commence the devil's power, the devil's origin, the whole living creation
would belong to the devil. By means of their splendour and glory the
ingenuous man Zarathushtra who spoke such good words, who was the
source of wisdom, who was born before Gotama, had such intercourse
with God. By means of their splendour and glory, the sun goes on his
path; by means of their splendour and glory the moon goes on her path;
by means of their splendour and glory the stars go on their path.[51]

At the soul's death, it returns to the *fravashi* and unites with it.[52] But even
though *fravashis* were immortal, they were not unchanging. Their relationship with the material creature over whom they watched could be affected
by its thoughts, words, and deeds. Possibly this was a later development
of Zoroastrian thought; yet upholding the relationship with your *fravashi*
was important not only because of how this could support you in the
struggle between your good and evil urges, but also because this increased
the amount of support that your *fravashi* could give you in the first place.

51 Müller, 205–206.
52 Carnoy, 868.

According to Zoroastrian teachings, the *fravashi*'s support could not be taken for granted:

> Similarly, the *fravashis* or Guardian Spirits are the most helpful genii, but on the condition that man propitiates them with sacrifices. When satisfied they are of indescribable help but once offended they are hard to deal with. They are to be approached with religious awe. They are to be feared rather than loved. This fear of the celestial beings may engender obedience in man, but not devotion. And devotion is the higher of the two virtues.[53]

Ritual Practice

WHEN WE LOOK AT the spiritual practices used by the Zoroastrians to engage with their guardian spirits, we discover something that will immediately interest Western practitioners of ritual magic. For Zoroastrians, the invocation of the *fravashi* was a crucial part of their spiritual life and practice.[54] Such an invocation was not at all an occult or secret practice, and it didn't require an extended period of purification or preparation.

As mentioned earlier, the ritual setup for a Zoroastrian is restricted to its most basic components. There is a sacred fire, always kept burning in each temple and devotee's house, which is ideally fed with sandalwood. There is incense to be sprinkled on its flames. There may be an offering of bread and milk. And there is the barsom, a bundle of twigs held in the hands as prayers are recited.[55] And that was it: the Zoroastrians repeatedly stated in their sacred books that these were the only accoutrements required to invoke one's holy daimon.

Just one of the many possible examples of prayers for invoking one's *fravashi* can be found in the Vendīdād:

53 Dhalla (1914), 79.
54 Lenormant, 199.
55 Carnoy, 868.

Invoke, O Zarathushtra! my Fravashi, who is Ahura Mazda, the greatest, the best, the fairest of all beings, the most solid, the most intelligent, the best formed, the highest in holiness, and whose soul is the Holy Word! Invoke, Zarathushtra! this creation of mine, which is Ahura Mazda. Zarathushtra imitated my words from me, and said: I invoke the Holy creation of Ahura Mazda.[56]

From a Western ritual perspective, it makes sense that we never encounter evocations but only invocations of the *fravashis* or other gods in Zoroastrian literature. This was a religion that tried to overcome the tribal cults of its nomadic origins by focusing mainly on prayer and devotion in its liturgical practice. And as the battle between good and evil raged at every level of creation – from the most divine to the most mundane – the powers of the *fravashi* were needed first and foremost where they mattered most: within each individual human being. Only if the devotee properly adored his *fravashi* and kept it close in thought, word and deed could he hope to achieve an increasing assimilation between his being and his *fravashi's* powers. The forces of the guardian spirit had to be drawn repeatedly into his being and soul to benefit fully from their divine power.

But it was not only one's own *fravashi* that could be invoked. Invocations of the *fravashis* of other people are also attested, especially those of powerful and righteous ancestors.[57]

Irrespective of the target of such an invocation – whether it was one's own *fravashi*, the *fravashi* of some righteous person, or the powers of the stars and gods – the invocation had to drip with profound reverence. And the praise and adoration was not limited to the target of the invocation, it was extended to everything involved in the ritual, both material and spiritual:

The following are the objects that come in for a share of invocation in the ritual: Haoma, Aeshma or the wood for the fire altar, Barsom or the sacred twigs, *zaothra* or libations, one's own soul and Fravashi, the

---

56 Horne, 144.
57 Horne, 148; Müller, 205.

Gathas, the chapters of the Yasna Haptanghaiti, meters, lines, words of the chapters of the Haptanghaiti, intellect, conscience, knowledge, and even sleep. Thus the creator and his creature, angel and man, ceremonial implements and scriptural texts are all alike made the objects of adoration and praise.[58]

The power that emanated from the prayers of the devotee dissolved the boundaries between the ritual's objective and subjective features. The ritual paraphernalia, one's soul, one's *fravashi*, one's consciousness, intellect, knowledge, and even sleep – they all merged and became one in prayer and reverence. Recognizable in this early Zoroastrian practice is a description of a state of deep devotional ecstasy.[59]

The importance of devotional ecstasy or trance is supported by the final characteristic of Zoroastrian ritual practice that we shall examine: *haoma*.

Besides this there was, despite Zoroaster's ban upon it, the sacrifice of *haoma* (= Skr. *soma*), an intoxicating plant of which the stems were crushed in a mortar and the juice strained off; this was presented before the fire and drunk by the officiating priest and his acolytes.[60]

There was much academic dispute regarding the botanical nature of *haoma* until, in the nineteenth century, it was finally identified convincingly as a species of the genus *Ephedra*. Drunk as an extract, the plant has a stimulant effect. The twigs held in prayer were also taken from the *haoma* plant. The name *haoma*, however, described not only the plant itself but also its divinity, that is, its *fravashi*.

We can now see a clearer picture emerge: We rediscovered an ancient Zoroastrian spiritual practice to create union with one's *fravashi*; the related instructions convey a unique synthesis of a tradition of liturgical invocations, combined with shamanistic trance techniques.

58 Dhalla, 80.
59 We will return to this essential aspect of Zoroastrian practice when we come to describe how to create the communion with our own holy daimon, particularly in the section devoted to joy.
60 Carnoy, 868.

Sacerdos Persicus

Let us visualize the scene. The Mazdean priest stands in the half-light of the temple, the sacred *haoma* twigs in his folded hands, reciting long prayers learned by heart as he stares, motionless, into the flames of the sacred fire. Clouds of incense rise from the flames, and, with his gaze deeply fixed on the blaze and the melody of the prayers flowing from his lips, the effect of the potion slowly takes effect.

It is revealing what Christian Rätsch, one of the leading botanists specializing in hallucinogens, had to say about the ancient spiritual goal of such practices (though the following quote describes that of inhaled psychoactive incense):

> It was in the smoke or odour of the incense that one realized the actions of gods, demons, angels, spirits, souls of the plants and others. They manifested within man once they were inhaled. This is why the smoke of certain sacred plants was breathed in or inhaled in order to give space in one's own body to the related spiritual beings.[61]

We can assume a similar purpose behind drinking the *haoma* potion, staring into flames for extended periods, and reciting the related prayers: to create a spirit vessel within one's own body for the powers one was attempting to invoke. Just as the ancient Egyptians and Greeks created spirit dwellings within statues, so it seems did the Zoroastrians within their own bodies, by invoking the powers of their *fravashis*, their personal spirit guardians.

✳   ✳

✳

61 Rätsch, 27.

AMONG THE ANCIENT GREEKS

Plato's Elements of the Soul

The unexamined life is not worth living.

– Socrates

PLATO COMPARES the human soul to a charioteer with two winged horses. The charioteer can be identified with the rational mind or reason; the noble horse with the *thumos*, a concept which we will explore shortly; and the unruly horse with our biological appetites, *eros*. When looking at the constitution of the human soul according to the ancient Greeks, this is as straightforward as we can make it.

Concerning the immortality of the soul this is enough; but about its form we must speak in the following manner. To tell what it really is would be a matter for utterly superhuman and long discourse, but it is within human power to describe it briefly in a figure; let us therefore speak in that way. We will liken the soul to the composite nature of a pair of winged horses and a charioteer. Now the horses and charioteers of the gods are all good and of good descent, but those of other races are mixed; and first the charioteer of the human soul drives a pair, and secondly one of the horses is noble and of noble breed, but the other quite the opposite in breed and character. Therefore in our case the driving is necessarily difficult and troublesome.[1]

1 Plato, *Phaedrus* 246a–b.

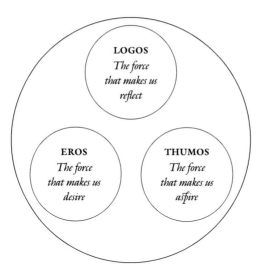

Let us now explore a slightly more detailed explanation of Plato's allegory, by John Michael Greer in *The Blood of the Earth*:

> One horse represents what we may as well call the biological self, guided by what Romantics called the instincts and Platonists called the appetites. The other horse, though, represents what the ancient Greeks called *thumos*, the spirited or irascible part of the self, the part that responds non-rationally to praise or blame from others, and more generally is guided by the pressures and influences of the community to which the individual belongs. To use a phrase Plato didn't, where the first horse is the biological self, the second horse can be described as the social self.[2]

To better understand the interplay between these two non-rational aspects of ourselves, I strongly recommend reading the full chapter in Greer's book. As simple as it might seem at first glance, the *thumos* is a critical part of the ancient Greek understanding of our soul. The word can best be translated in English as 'spiritedness' or 'courage.' Etymologically the word has an association with the breath or the blood, and it is also used to ex-

---

2 Greer, 38f.

press the human desire for social recognition. Thus the nobler of the two dominating non-rational driving forces in the human soul is enmeshed with the social environment in which a person was raised.

As far as I know, there is no analogy to this idea in either Christianity, Judaism or Kabbalah. What we find here is a term that describes the non-rational and nonverbal patterns in our behaviour which are shaped and emotionally charged by the social communities into which we are born. It is through the *thumos* that the collective being of a tribe or society leaves a significant imprint on the individual. In other words, it is in the *thumos* that our microcosm reflects our social macrocosm.

This explains why, according to Plato, the *thumos* represents the noble horse. Our capacity for nobility, honour, glory, virtue, and even our basic values are all the results of our social norms and interactions, condensed and imprinted into the *thumos* of our soul. Following its impulses, even if the results were angry, violent, and untamed, was the only way to achieve social status. It was also the power that drove warriors into battle.[3]

The ancient Greek *thumos*, however, was not a mere social construct: it was a real life force, guarded over and replenished by the gods themselves. In fact, when the *thumos* left the body of a person it meant their immediate death:

> After Dioreus had been fatally hit 'he fell backwards in the dust...while he blew forth his *thumos*.' (...) Ajax hit Sarpedon's comrade-in-arms Epikles, who 'like an acrobat fell down from the high wall, and the *thumos* left his bones. (...) Diomedes slew the sons of Phaenops and 'took out the *thumos* from both.'[4]

A person dominated by their *thumos* was destined to become a warrior of high social status in life. On the other hand, the talents of a person dominated by the other horse, the unruly one, disposed him more to becoming something like a successful merchant. It is worth noting that the word *eros* has become overgrown with romantic associations in the last two

---

3 For more on the relationship between the *thumos* and warrior fury, look at the idea of *menos* as something located within the *thumos*, in Bremmer, 58f.

4 Bremmer, 75.

thousand years. Its archaic origin, however, referred to the much more basic and raw desire for sustenance and material life. Here is how Plato describes this lower part of the soul in his *Timaeus*:

> The part of the soul which desires meats and drinks and the other things of which it has need by reason of the bodily nature, they placed between the midriff and the boundary of the navel, contriving in all this region a sort of manger for the food of the body; and there they bound it down like a wild animal which was chained up with man, and must be nourished if man was to exist.[5]

In many aspects the *eros*, or *epithumetikon* as opposed to the *thumetikon*, can be imagined as the complete opposite of the *thumos*. Whereas the *thumos* rules over the positive (social) emotions, the *eros* yearns to set free the (biological) desires and urges. Whereas the *thumos* represents the vitalizing force of spiritedness, the *eros* reveals our basic cravings – our appetites, as the Greeks would say – for food, sex, and shelter. The *thumos* was viewed as masculine in nature, whereas the *eros* was feminine. We might map *thumos* and *eros* onto Maslow's hierarchy of human needs by viewing *thumos* as the higher, social needs, and *eros* as the source and container of the physiological 'life energy' – a term in which sense the word *eros* has often been used in Greek philosophy.

As we can see, both horses had a place and function in the human soul, and when a healthy mind holds the reins, it can drive the 'chariot' forwards. The *logos*, therefore – the charioteer in the analogy – was of utmost importance. This was where intellect had its throne, and from which reason and logic emerged. Whereas the horses pulled in the directions of social status and biological needs, the *logos* desired nothing but learning and wisdom. Only by means of this mental function was the soul able to balance the impulses and urges of the two winged horses. According to Plato, people dominated by the *logos* or *logistikon* made great philosophers or politicians.

5 Plato, *Timaeus* 3.38.

Nous – The Ancient Higher Self

A T THIS point we encounter a philosophical problem that particularly interested the ancient Greeks. The faculties of the soul – *eros*, *thumos* and *logos* – must necessarily be extremely biased. *Eros* is driven by the sensual impressions of the world and our bodily appetites, while *thumos* is driven by social norms and expectations. *Logos*, the pure capacity for mental reflection, can generate nothing by itself: It can only process the data provided by the *eros* and *thumos*, and this data is filtered by them before the *logos* receives it.

What so worried the Greeks was that, while our physical senses do collect raw data about the reality that surrounds us, the tripartite soul cannot process this data without significantly altering or biasing it. What we truly touch, hear, smell, and see is not what we perceive and process in our mind. For this raw information to reach our mind, it first has to be processed by the inner organs of our soul. Thus we are caught in a world where the faculties of our soul distort perception according to their nature, depriving us of the ability to perceive nature as it truly is.

Here is another way to understand this problem. Think of your mind as a traveller in a strange land, who does not speak the native language. Thankfully this traveller always has two translators at his side, though neither is reliable. One of them has a tendency to focus unnecessarily on physical appetites and desires, while the other is obsessed with social status and is constantly on the lookout for chances to prove his courage and nobility. As the traveller has no means to communicate directly with the people around him, his interactions are always distorted by the personal preferences of his two translators. By the end of his sojourn, the chances are high that our traveller has learned more about his two translators than the country through which he was travelling. Such is the situation of the charioteer (the *logos*) when it comes to objectively perceiving and making sense of the world. It is dependent on two functions that don't provide it with accurate data. To make things even worse, later philosophers showed that there is no way to correct the data once it has been filtered through *thumos* and *eros*. So how can we know what really happens beyond the reach of our senses? Well, luckily there is a fourth function of the soul, one we haven't yet examined. It is called the *nous*, the faculty of the mind we can perhaps understand as being similar to intuition.

It is the function of *nous* that allows us to understand nature in an undistorted way and to achieve true insights about reality. While physical reality is constantly changing, and while our perceptions will always be biased due to their being filtered through *eros* and *thumos*, the *nous* ever remains pure and untouched by the tides of matter. Thus *nous* not only allows us to piece together the information received through our senses in an undistorted way, but it also provides us with a higher form of insight and knowledge. *Nous* can be translated both as understanding and intuition.

Plato uses two metaphors to describe the way the *nous* functions. In his metaphor of the sun, he compares it to the sunlight that helps our eyes see. And in his Socratic dialogue *Meno*, he explains *nous* as those ideas embroidered into a man's soul which he might recall from previous lives. Either way, Plato makes it clear that this light which helps us see, or these ideas which help us remember, come from the immortal part of our soul; all other parts of it vanish at our death. Both metaphors illustrate how the *nous* surpasses both the material and human realms. It allows its human carriers to ascend beyond the limitations of illusory reality and to glimpse behind the veils of matter. *Nous* was often understood as the divine or spiritual assistance that humans receive to help them comprehend reality. It is the living spiritual force that allows us to draw true reasoning from flawed perceptions. Because of this, it was also said that *nous* as a divine principle is something that could never mix with any other substance, but instead effortlessly penetrated all created things. Anaxagoras of Clazomenae, born circa 500 BCE, had the following to say about the *nous*:

> All other things partake in a portion of everything, while *nous* is infinite and self-ruled, and is mixed with nothing, but is alone, itself by itself. For if it were not by itself, but were mixed with anything else, it would partake in all things if it were mixed with any; for in everything there is a portion of everything, as has been said by me in what goes before, and the things mixed with it would hinder it, so that it would have power over nothing in the same way that it has now being alone by itself. For it is the thinnest of all things and the purest, and it has all knowledge about everything and the greatest strength; and *nous* has power over all things, both greater and smaller, that have soul.[6]

According to Anaxagoras it was the *nous* itself that gave order and intelligence to creation. And as it wasn't bound to any material shell, it existed on many levels. Humans were understood to partake in the benefits of *nous*, yet at the same time the celestial spheres had their own *nous* or understanding.

---

6 https://www.ellopos.net/elpenor/greek-texts/ancient-greece/anaxagoras-/nous/.asp

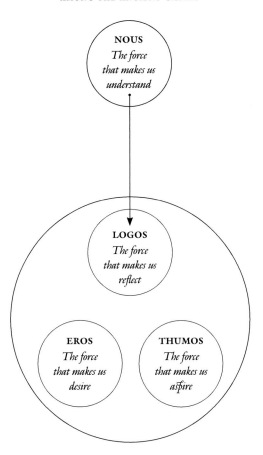

The spiritual significance of this concept becomes yet more obvious when we consider the etymological connections between the words *nous* (mind), *noesis* (understanding, from *noein*, to perceive), and *gnosis* (divine knowledge). Let's pause and consider what we have found: an ancient idea of an all-permeating force too subtle to be contained or confined by any type of substance. Nevertheless, it is in the nature of this force to attach itself to individual objects and entire celestial realms alike, and to grant them the power of true insight and the ability to create meaning. The name of this force is sometimes translated as 'intellect' and sometimes as 'understanding,' but most commonly simply as 'mind.' And it exists separate from the mental and spiritual functions of the being to which it attaches itself; it is something entirely different from *logos*, *eros* or *thumos*.

Over two thousand years later, this same concept is still an integral part of Western ritual magic. It is still called 'intelligence,' and we find many occult writers and practitioners, among them Agrippa of Nettesheim, explaining its function in great detail:

> It is affirmed by Magicians, that there are certain tables of numbers distributed to the seven planets, which they call the sacred tables of the planets, endowed with many, and very great vertues of the Heavens, in as much as they represent that divine order of Celestiall numbers, impressed upon Celestials by the Ideas of the divine mind, by means of the soul of the world, and the sweet harmony of those Celestiall rayes, signifying according to the proportion of effigies, supercelestiall Intelligencies, which can no other way be expressed, than by the marks of numbers, and Characters. For materiall numbers, and figures can do nothing in the mysteries of hid things, but representatively by formall numbers, and figures, as they are governed, and informed by intelligencies, and divine numerations, which unite the extreams of the matter, and spirit to the will of the elevated soul, receiving through great affection, by the Celestiall power of the operator, a power from God, applyed through the soul of the universe, and observations of Celestiall constellations, to a matter fit for a form, the mediums being disposed by the skill, and industry of Magicians (...).[7]

The word 'Intelligencies' describes the same concept as the Greek *nous*: this is a strand of occult philosophy that has survived for nearly two thousand years. The 'celestial intellect' of the planetary squares is the living, divine mind (*nous*) of the planet itself. This explains why its *nous* cannot be expressed other than through numbers and figures: they are the most abstract ways for us to think about things, and as distinct from physical substance as it is possible for us to get. Just as the Greeks considered the

---

7 Agrippa, *Three Books of Occult Philosophy*, Book II, chapter XXII.

function of the *nous* in the human soul to be to unite the ephemeral nature of matter with the eternal spirit behind it, Agrippa states that the celestial intelligence of each planet can unite the extremes of matter and spirit. Considering the above, it is of no surprise to find a strong tendency in Plato's writing to deify the spiritual nature of *nous*.[8] According to Plato, *nous* was implanted in man as something divine, as 'a daimon in man.'[9] By following Plato's principle of giving each thing the food most natural to it,[10] a man could increasingly align the state of his own soul with the nature of his *daimon*. All that was needed was to lead his life according to the principles of divine understanding:

> But he who has been earnest in the love of knowledge and of true wis-
> dom, and has exercised his intellect [i.e. his *nous*] more than any other
> part of him, must have thoughts immortal and divine, if he attains
> truth, and in so far as human nature is capable of sharing in immortal-
> ity, he must altogether be immortal; and since he is ever cherishing the
> divine power, and has the divinity within him in perfect order, he will
> be perfectly happy.[11]

What we discover here is a process of co-creation between the external forces of the *nous* and the internal forces of the human *logos*. A harmoniza- tion between the two is achieved only through approaching them togeth- er. Just as the *daimon* of the *nous* directs us 'upward from earth to kinship with heaven,'[12] so must our own *logos* tame the horses of *thumos* and *eros* to ascend this ladder by actively pursuing knowledge and true wisdom. The spiritual relationship between the *daimon* of the *nous* and the human *logos* is an interdependent one: even though they are separated by nature, the true fulfilment of their nature can be achieved only through each other.

8 Burkert, 331.
9 Burkert, 328.
10 *Timaeus*, 90a.
11 *Timaeus*, 90a.
12 *Timaeus*, 90a.

Someone once said to me, 'It is in the nature of our holy daimon to, from the day of our birth, constantly pray down to us. We can meet it halfway, though, by starting to pray upwards to it.' We can still hear the echo of Plato's thoughts in this analogy, Plato who described humans as 'plants of heaven on earth.'[13] The intricate connection of the human soul with the celestial sphere is further strengthened by Plato's assertion that each soul has its own native star from which it has come and to which it will return after death.[14]

> And having made it [the soul mixture], he [the Demiurge] divided the whole mixture into souls equal in number to the stars, and assigned each soul to a star; and having there placed them as in a chariot, he showed them the nature of the universe, and declared to them the laws of destiny (...). He who lived well during his appointed time was to return and dwell in his native star, and there he would have a blessed and congenial existence.[15]

Thus the *daimon* of the *nous* can be understood as a mediator between the earthly realm and the celestial sphere from which we stem and to which we will ultimately return. This view was, of course, echoed by Crowley in his famous aphorism, 'Every man and every woman is a star.' We could even go so far as to view the *daimon* of the *nous* as a living, spiritual chain that connects man to his eternal higher self. The ancient Greeks viewed such a mediating function as being the essential nature of their *daimones*.[16]

✳

13 Burkert, 328.
14 *Timaeus*, 42b; Burkert, 328.
15 *Timaeus*, 41 d–e.
16 *Symposium*, 202e.

The Early Greek Idea of the Daimon

T HE ORIGINAL technical meaning and the etymological origin of the Greek δαίμων (*daimon*) is lost in the darkness of ancient history. Our understanding of the word, 'a lowly spiritual being of a preponderant-ly dangerous and evil character'[17] is strongly influenced by the works of Plato and Xenocrates, which were composed between 396–313 BCE. The meaning of the word *daimon* before then, however, was much more ambiguous. To get a better understanding of its meaning before the time of Plato we must scrape away three distinct layers of ideological sedi-ment that have accreted to the word *daimon* over the last two and a half thousand years. According to Walter Burkert[18] and many other scholars, the early use of the word did not specify any specific category of spiritual

17 Burkert, 179.
18 Burkert, 180.

beings, nor was any relationship with any god implied. Nor did it imply anything about the *daimon*'s moral character. The early use of the term *daimon* is best illustrated with a few examples taken from ancient Greek literature:

> In the *Iliad*, the gods assembled on Mount Olympus can be called *daimones*, and Aphrodite leads the way ahead of Helen as *daimon*. A hero may rush headlong 'like *daimon* and still be called god-like, *isotheos*. Conversely, the demons that fly from Pandora's jar are personified 'illnesses', *nousoi*, but are not called *daimones*; the death-bringing spirits of destruction, *keres*, are called *theoi*, as are the Erinyes in Aeschylus. Possession, too, is the work of a god.[19]

Originally, then, the word *daimon* did not describe a particular category of spiritual beings, but rather a peculiar mode of activity.[20] Being under the influence of a *daimon* was to be in a certain state. Just as we distinguish the states of trance and gnosis from the state of the normal waking mind, so the ancient Greeks used the word *daimon* to indicate a specific state of being that was different from normal everyday consciousness. This state was not confined to human experience, for almost anything could be affected by it: humans, heroes, and even gods.

> Even if all statements about it [the *daimon*] may be very difficult, the definition that helps to approach the topic is one which understands it as an immense driving force, neither good nor evil, and which increases the level of experience through a dangerous tension.[21]

Unfortunately, unlike Plato's triad of *thumos*, *eros* and *logos*, the ancient Greeks never seem to describe the 'immense driving force' of the *daimon* in any abstract or generalized fashion. The word *daimon* seems to have been so familiar to them, and its various nuances so well known, that its intended meaning always seems to have been understandable by context

19 Burkert, 180.
20 Burkert, 180.
21 Müller-Sternberg, 82.

alone, without ever requiring further explanation. What we do know is that the *daimon* always represented some sort of occult force, some nameless power that overcame people like a dark wave and withdrew them from the bright lights of social encounters. Under the influence of the *daimon*, the causes of a person's actions became arcane and veiled to the human realm. Something took hold of them and started to work through them. It was the power of the *daimon* that could turn any hitherto self-determined being into a willing agent of some occult force.[22]

> For daimon (...) is more reproach than praise, and therefore certainly does not mean divine; it is used when the speaker does not understand what the addressee is doing and why he is doing it. Daimon is occult power, a force that drives man forward where no agent can be named. The individual feels as it were that the tide is with him, he acts with the daimon, *syn daimoni*, or else when everything turns against him, he stands against the daimon, *pros daimona* (...).[23]

With such an interpretation of the term, the importance of being on good terms with one's *daimon* becomes obvious. It was an occult, invisible force which could be perceived only indirectly through its actions and effects. It was the driving power behind the tides of fate and thus behind the fortune of a person's life.

Now we can understand why the average man experienced his *daimon* not only as deeply uncanny but mostly as something to be feared. It was not because it was attached to any specific type of spiritual being or moral category, but simply because it was completely unknown and beyond human control. The *daimon* appeared out of darkness, took hold of the beings it used as its agents for a period of time, then disappeared again.

A man could not control whether he was the subject of a good or an evil *daimon*, which made for fortune or misfortune. This is how the terms 'good' and 'evil' *daimon*, the *agathodaimon* and *kakodaimon*, need to be understood. Originally they did not refer to different categories of spiritual

22 Müller-Sternberg, 37.
23 Burkert, 180.

56

beings, but rather the effects, for better or worse, that the occult tides of the *daimon* would have on one's personal life.

The *daimon* defined the quality of one's fate.[24] It was only at a later point in the evolution of Greek philosophy that this view of the *daimon* developed into discrete categories of spiritual beings who could take control of our lives.

Whether he is happy or unhappy is not something which lies in man's control; the happy man is the one who has a good daimon, *eudaimon*, in contrast to the unhappy man, the *kakodaimon, dysdaimon*. (...) A general belief in spirits is not expressed by the term *daimon* until the fifth century.[25]

The Socratic Daimonion

Serve the gods and you will experience how they are looking after you and that they are sending you mentors.

– Socrates, *Mem*.I 4.18, in Volquardsen, 18

WITH SOCRATES AND PLATO, the idea of a personal *daimon* becomes part of the historical record, though most likely the notion had already been around for quite some time.[26] While Socrates' confident claim of a personal *daimonion* that advised him throughout his life ultimately led to his death sentence, he refused to give details about this being or inner voice during his apologia at court. Indeed, his *daimonion* had advised him not to defend himself; thus he appeared unprepared during his trial and even rejected an apologia offered to him by the speaker Lysias.[27]

---

24 Müller-Sternberg, 57.
25 Burkert, 181.
26 Burkert, 181.
27 du Prel, 125.

The most interesting aspect of Socrates' *daimonion*, which has been widely researched, is that it would never encourage him towards any action, but only warn and restrain him. Or as Plato put it:

> To confine the daimonion coerces me, to create it refuses me.[28]

What exactly do we know about Socrates' understanding of his personal *daimonion* – a concept that despite the dreadful sentence it brought upon Socrates became so widespread and well known in later centuries? First, it must be noted that Socrates always used a particular Greek word to denote this supporting inner agency: he called it his *daimonion*, never his *daimon*. The difference lies in the gender of the noun. Socrates chose a neuter gender, indicating that he viewed it as a daimonic something or even a divine sign, and not necessarily a conscious entity in itself.[29] We can only assume that this specific verbal expression was grounded in his inner experience. The charge that he faced in his trial was of introducing new gods and not devoting himself to the old ones. In light of this, his choice of a neuter noun to describe his enigmatic inner voice becomes more understandable.

Furthermore, Socrates clarifies that his inner voice wasn't something he got access to through conscious practice, spiritual devotion, or any types of religious ritual and had been with him since childhood.[30] In this sense in particular, Socrates' *daimonion* exemplifies the function of an inner guardian. His inner voice actively watched over the choices he made in life, irrespective of their seeming significance or insignificance. Its only mode of operation was to ensure that Socrates did not stray from the path assigned him by the gods. The *daimonion* was the inner guardian that made sure Socrates fulfilled the pattern of his fate – and a significant destiny it was, for he inspired the entire Western philosophical tradition.

The ancient notion of the term *daimon* as an occult force responsible for making a man's life happy or miserable is perhaps reflected in the consistent quality Socrates ascribed to his inner voice. Both the ancient

28 Plato, *Theaetet* 7, acc. to du Prel.
29 du Prel, 122.
30 Apol. Plato 31; Volquardsen, 8.

daimon and Socrates' neutral inner *daimonion* are occult forces intrinsically connected to one's quality of life. But whereas the *daimon* took hold of people in mysterious ways and made them act under its influence without seeming reason, the *daimonion* proactively and consciously warned Socrates not to stray from his assigned path. The reason for the difference lies in the conscious bond that Socrates had made with his inner guardian. Whereas the average man experienced his *daimon* only as a force outside of his control – as a blow of fate or a run of good luck – Socrates experienced his *daimonion* as an intimate inner relationship that he valued so much he didn't hesitate to call it divine.[31]

> Even you, Euthydem, will realize that my faith in the daimonion and divine mentorship is true, if you'll honour and serve the gods and realize them in their deeds instead of waiting to perceive them incarnated face to face.[32]

As this quote demonstrates, Socrates believed that the sort of relationship he had with his *daimonion* was accessible to anyone. Even though he had been granted this gift in childhood, he offers clear guidance on how to develop this inner contact: by understanding the world and all experiences within it as direct expressions of the gods, by recognizing the divine spirits according to their deeds and creations, and by not waiting to be granted a direct vision of them. Thus next to dreams and oracles[33] any experience in life can become an encounter with the divine. Hidden in the book of nature is the voice of our *daimonion*. Interestingly, there is a modern parallel to this explanation of attaining communion with one's *daimonion* that we should highlight here. In the magical tradition of the Golden Dawn, the initiate needs to take several oaths when progressing through liminal grades such as Adeptus Minor and Adeptus Major. The final oath to be taken, when the adept is aspiring to journey from Chesed (7 = 4) to Binah (8 = 2) and to cross the Abyss, is the Oath of the Master of the Temple, and it concludes with the following statement:

31 Volquardsen, 8, 9.
32 Socrates *Mem.* IV, 3, 13, in Volquardsen, 18.
33 Volquardsen, 18.

I swear to interpret every phenomenon as a particular dealing of God with my soul.[34]

This is strikingly similar to Socrates' guidance on how to achieve communion with one's *daimonion* or divine mentor: to comprehend the gods in the deeds they perform in the world that surrounds us rather than waiting until they reveal themselves. Some twenty-five centuries after Socrates drank the hemlock, the same voice still calls to the spiritual seeker, one that the ancient Kabbalists came to express simply as 'Kether is in Malkuth and Malkuth is in Kether, but after another manner.'

The Deification of Man

HAVING EXPLORED the ancient origin of the Greek word *daimon* and Socrates' particular take on the *daimonion*, we return to Plato, with whose analogy of the soul we began this chapter. It is in Plato's writings, and in his unparalleled influence on both Western and Arabic thought, that we discover the foundation of the concept of the holy daimon as it evolved in later centuries.

Since Plato and through him, religion has been essentially different from what it had been before. For the Greeks as we know them since Homer, religion had always meant acceptance of reality, in a naive and yet adult way, acceptance of a reality that included corporeality, transitoriness, and destruction, in heroic defiance or in tragic insight. Through Plato reality is made unreal in favour of an incorporeal, unchangeable other world which is to be regarded as primary. The ego is concentrated in an immortal soul which is alien to the body and captive in it. 'Flight from the world' is a watchword which actually occurs in Plato.[35]

34 Crowley, 180.
35 Burkert, 322.

With Plato, and for the first time in Greek philosophy, truth and ontological reality shifted outside of corporeal reality. Whereas gods had previously mingled with humans and changed their forms to take animal, plant, stone, and marine forms, now this direct way of experiencing the divine through the manifest world began to be replaced by a more abstract conception of divinity. Now true being and ontological reality were to be found only behind the veils and analogies of corporeal nature.

Plato derived many of his original thoughts from mathematics.[36] Fascinated by the fact that humans couldn't experience mathematical truths directly through their physical senses but instead had to leverage their rational minds to pierce through the effects caused by hidden laws, Plato proceeded to apply the principles of mathematics to philosophy. The result was a revolutionary view about where truth was to be found. Mathematicians and seekers of wisdom alike had to use the force of their *logos* to pierce through the phenomena of the material world and discover the eternal ideas and living substance hidden behind them. Other philosophers, such as Parmenides, had already assumed a deeper, timeless ontological reality behind the veil of nature; however, it was Plato who broadened and diversified this idea and postulated that there was not one absolute source of being beyond matter, but as many sources as there were beings.[37] Just as each human being had unique facial features, so there was an eternal idea assigned to them in which they alone participated.[38] Thus amongst the ancient Greeks it was Plato who introduced the philosophical idea of deifying all beings through a direct personal bond with divine reality.

At the same time he made the human soul immortal – or at least the part of it connected to the eternal idea from which it had emerged. Plato states that in his day it was a common belief that the soul, when it left its body at the moment of death, was grasped by the wind and diffused in all directions into the sky.[39] Even today traces of this ancient belief persist in the myth, still alive in some parts of Europe, that when a man dies by

36 Burkert, 322.
37 Rohde, 278.
38 Burkert, 323.
39 Rohde, 264.

hanging a storm rises and takes his soul away – probably in the form of the storm ghosts of the Wild Hunt.[40]

Plato took essential elements of the traditions of the mystery schools, as well as earlier ones such as the Orphic tradition, and combined them with his own metaphysical concept of a realm of pure and eternal ideas beyond physical matter.[41] In his cosmology, the fixed stars were the closest physical representation of the realm of the eternal ideas, as they were considered unchangeable, divine living beings. Below them were the planets, which partook more strongly in the principles of creation, as they could be observed to move, changing and developing through time. Below the planets was a vast sphere filled with *daimones* or gods.

The status of these divine beings, sometimes called gods and sometimes referred to as *daimones*, was considerably lower in Plato's cosmology than in earlier Greek thought. However, these divine beings, together with the influence of the stars and planets, were still viewed as causing all created things to take their respective forms and states of being,[42] while the *daimones* were active mediators operating between the fixed, starry sphere, the moving planetary one, and the sublunary human realm.

> For such is the nature of *daimones*: they stand in the middle between gods and men, they are 'interpreters and ferrymen' who communicate the messages and gifts from men to the gods and from gods to men, prayers and sacrifices from one side, commands and recompenses from the other.[43]

Earlier we investigated the *nous*, a principle in the human soul that allows man to free himself from the bonds of matter and reach out into the transcendental realm of truth and eternal being. Just as the Greek gods can affect the physical realm but don't belong there, so the *nous* can penetrate all physical matter and speak to man in his mind and heart, yet it doesn't belong there. The highest function of the human soul has thus

40 Rohde, 264.
41 Rohde, 279.
42 Burkert, 328, 332.
43 Burkert, 331.

itself become a daimon: an intermediary being building a living bridge between the man caught in matter and the eternal star assigned to him at birth. By deifying the *nous*, Plato laid the foundation for the philosophical and occult tradition that knows of a personal and immortal divine being assigned to and watching over each man and woman.[44] This tutelary genius (Latin for Greek *daimon*) remains invisible and veiled as the personal *nous-daimon* while humans are alive. During this time, interaction takes place through inner dialogue and divine intuition. But after death the guardian *daimon* becomes perceptible as an entity, a living being, in its own right, though still bound to and yet still separate from the incarnated being that was its charge. Plato describes this clearly in both *Phaedo* and *Laws*, and the relevant sections are worth quoting in full:

> And so it is said that after death, the tutelary genius of each person, to whom he had been allotted in life, leads him to a place where the dead are gathered together; then they are judged and depart to the other world with the guide whose task it is to conduct thither those who come from this world; and when they have there received their due and remained through the time appointed, another guide brings them back after many long periods of time.[45]

> Cronos was aware of the fact that no human being (...) is capable of having irresponsible control of all human affairs without becoming filled with pride and injustice; so, pondering this fact, he then appointed as kings and rulers for our cities, not men, but beings of a race that was nobler and more divine, namely, daimons. He acted just as we now do in the case of sheep and herds of tame animals: we do not set oxen as rulers over oxen, or goats over goats, but we, who are of a nobler race, ourselves rule over them. In like manner the God, in his love for humanity, set over us at that time the nobler race of daimons who, with much comfort to themselves and much to us, took charge of us and

44 Burkert, 328–331.
45 Plato, *Phaedo* 107d/e.

furnished peace and modesty and orderliness and justice without stint, and thus made the tribes of men free from feud and happy.[46]

The Evil Daimon

I N THE HISTORY of the Western occult, we come across several accounts of a being complementary to the *daimon* of *nous*, the so-called evil daimon. Whereas the good genius helps us break through the biased veils of sensual perception and reconnect with the eternal realm of truth and being, the evil daimon tries to hinder us in these efforts and pull us back behind the veils of matter. We have already encountered the following explanation of this evil daimon in the *Divine Pymander* of the *Corpus Hermeticum*:

But to the foolish, and evil, and wicked, and envious, and covetous, and murderous, and profane, I am far off, giving place to the revenging Demon, which applying unto him the sharpness of fire, tormenteth such a man sensible, and armeth him the more to all wickedness, that he may obtain the greater punishment. And such an one never ceaseth, having unfulfilled desires, and unsatisfiable concupiscences, and always fighting in darkness; for the Demon always afflicts and tormenteth him continually, and increaseth the fire upon him more and more.[47]

But from these I remain distant – the thoughtless and evil and wicked and envious and greedy and violent and irreverent – giving way to the avenging demon who [wounds the evil person], assailing him sensibly with the piercing fire and thus arming him the better for lawless deeds so that greater vengeance may befall him. Such a person does not cease longing after insatiable appetites, struggling in the darkness without satisfaction. [This] tortures him and makes the fire grow upon him all the more.[48]

46 Plato, *Laws* 713 c–e.
47 *The Divine Pymander*, Book II, 56, 57, in Westcott, 27, 28.
48 *The Hermetica*, Copenhaver (1992), 5.

In *De occulta philosophia,* Agrippa describes nine orders of evil spirits counterbalancing the nine celestial orders of angels. The last rung of this infernal ladder he reserved for the evil daimon assigned to each person:

> Moreover the Tempters and Ensnarers have the last place, one of which is present with every man, which we therefore call the evil Genius, and their Prince is Mammon, which is interpreted as covetousness (...).[49]

In chapter XXVI of the same book, Agrippa details an Arabian method of drawing out the names of the good and evil genii from one's astrological chart – a topic to which we shall return.

Given the widespread belief in a twofold daimonic presence within each human being, let's see what we can learn from the ancient Greeks about its origins. As we have already seen, in the early stages of Greek philosophy there is little if any evidence to be found of the concept of an evil daimon: the *daimon* was considered an undifferentiated occult force that struck from the darkness and which had the power to alter a person's fate in all manner of directions. This force was beyond human control: even gods and heroes were affected by it. We have also seen that the *daimon* was defined not by its morality, but by its agency. The *daimon* didn't put good or evil thoughts into the mind of man; it seized him and enchanted him in a strange rhythm that had the power to change the tides of his life.[50] This Homeric understanding of the *daimon* is different from what we generally mean by daimon today: our sort of daimon is first attested in the works of Xenocrates, who was writing several hundred years after Homer.[51]

Both Xenocrates and Aristotle attended Plato's Academy in Athens. But whereas for Aristotle mathematics and science were unquestionably the correct basis for philosophy, having little time for his mentor Plato's old-fashioned mysticism, Xenocrates worked on investigating the mystery

---

49 Agrippa, Book III, chapter XVIII.
50 Müller-Sternberg, 244.
51 We should, however, bear in mind that Xenocrates' views on daimons may have reflected widespread folk beliefs that were already centuries old in his day.

cults and traditional religion of the ancient Greeks and integrating them with Plato's occult teachings.[52]

The character of Xenocrates thought was much rougher and more concrete than both Plato and many of his successors. Whereas Plato was deliberately ambiguous as to whether the highest god was a philosophical principle or a living being, Xenocrates called him 'Zeus' and saw him sitting on a throne next to the All-Mother, who personified the soul of all created things.[53] This tendency of Xenocrates to simplify complex spiritual matters is also found in his approach to the daimonic.

Before Xenocrates, there had been no articulated doctrine of the daimonic. Though it appears as an uncanny and elusive presence in both the early epics, and is dealt with as such in the teachings of Socrates, Plato, and many other Greek philosophers, it had never been given a defined place, function, or definition. It was Xenocrates, with his love of objectifying the abstract, who first set the daimonic on a more concrete footing.[54]

Like Plato, Xenocrates divided the cosmos into three concentric spheres. The most primal gods were the monad ('the One') and the dyad ('Two' or 'Otherness') who ruled over the first, outermost sphere. Under them was the sphere of the celestial stars and visible planets, which were considered to be divine, living beings. Under these, and separated by the sphere of the Moon, was the earthly realm, which was filled with a multitude of different spiritual forces and beings. This last, 'sublunary' realm according to Xenocrates was the sphere of the *daimones*.[55]

Xenocrates' view of the 'evil daimon' was a strange hybrid of Plato's ideas about the nature of evil and his own. This hybrid proved exceptionally hardy, as it shaped western beliefs about evil for the next two millennia. Plato himself was not particularly clear about the origin of evil, though on this subject 'various dialogues drop scattered hints.'[56] Nevertheless, most scholars agree that he ascribed evil's origin to the nature of matter itself. As we have already discussed, for Plato, *eros*, being fixated on fulfilling its

52 Heinze, VII.
53 Heinze, VIII.
54 Heinze, VIX.
55 Heinze, VIII.
56 Chilcott, 27.

material desires, necessarily biases perception, logic, and the influence of the all-pervading *nous*.[57] But why should matter distort the purity of the *nous*, the sublime and good? Plato had an intriguing explanation. According to him, the first beings were the divine ideas, which were the absolutely pure, sublime, and perfectly defined forms from which everything else in creation would emerge. The limitation of the unlimited into specific ideas is the basic principle of the emergence of god into creation. The nature of evil can, therefore, be explained in the following way:

> [It is] the failure of the particular to represent the idea, or (...) the failure of the unlimited to participate rightly in the limited. That is to say, evil has a purely negative existence. (...) [A] thing is good in so far as it represents the idea, evil in so far as it fails to do so, and the varying kinds and degrees of good and evil represent the degrees and kinds of approximation to or divergence from the ideal standard. The problem of the origin of evil, therefore, may now be stated thus: 'What is it which causes the particular to diverge from the idea?' The answer generally given to this question (...) is that there is an inherent incompatibility between the idea and matter; the former must always struggle to subdue the latter, and in many cases partially fail.[58]

According to Plato, evil is any lack of equivalence or analogy between a divine idea and its manifestation – and physical matter is inherently unable to represent divine ideas perfectly. The difference between divine ideas and their worldly expressions is the space where all evil emerges.

Traces of this line of thought appear several centuries later in the Safed school of Kabbalah, out of which Lurianic Kabbalah developed, in the concept of the breaking of the vessels that set divine forces free in an uncontrolled manner which thus gave birth to the origin of evil as the Qliphothic forces. This cosmic accident was caused by the inadequacy of the vessel of Geburah to capture and sustain the divine light.

---

57 Heinze, 27.
58 Chilcott, 28

The evil daimon is therefore what distorts the reflection of the primal ideas in man. Unlike the *nous*, however, it does not have any ontological reality of its own. The evil daimon is not a being in its own right; it is the imperfect alignment between the divine and the material. If anything, the evil daimon could be viewed as the unruliness of matter itself, the fractiousness of the appetites that prevents the good from unfolding in its perfect shape in the sublunary realm.

The purpose of man can be thought of as the work of a stonemason: to set free an invisible shape caught in rough matter, to bring to light a perfect idea in a world of unruly senses. The *logos* is man's chisel, the *thumos* his hammer, the *eros* the stone he works on, and the *nous* the light that shines in his mind. A good sculptor is guided by vision and well provisioned by the skill of his craft. A bad sculptor, however, is not necessarily led astray by an evil daimon; more likely he is simply insufficiently skilled to tame his stone's unruliness.

> To each human being is assigned at the moment of his birth a good spirit, his guide through the mysteries of life. We must not believe that the spirit is evil and can harm our lives; he is good, and there is no evil in him. Every good must be good. But those who are bad themselves, who have bad characters and make a muddle out of their lives, managing everything badly through their own foolishness (...) they make a divine being responsible and call it 'bad', while they are actually bad themselves.[59]

At the end of our journey into ancient Greek philosophy, we have discovered a straightforward, yet powerful idea – though of course it is but one voice in the philosophical choir of ancient thought. The idea is this: that from the moment of birth until we leave our mortal bodies, a good being is assigned to us, watching over and supporting all our efforts to draw down the divine into matter and so make matter sublime. Possibly some of our failures to do this may be down to some member of the evil daimonic horde which shares the sublunary realm with us. Yet none of

---

59 Menander, 342–291 BCE, in Luck, 172.

these *daimones* is personally attached to us, unlike the good *daimon* of our *nous*. None of them are bound into the nature of our soul.

However, more often than not, our failures are not due to any evil daimon: they are all our own work. For it is exceptionally hard to become what only humans can become: a bridge which allows for undistorted communication between *nous* and matter, one flowing into the other. Yet man can be such a bridge, standing in the service of what passes through him, unconditional and free from all appetites and desires. Man can be a noble soul.

✳   ✳

✳

PART II

MEMORY

COMMUNION WITH
MY HOLY DAIMON

T HIS PART OF THE BOOK relates my own experiences of creating
a communion with my holy daimon. The following pages contain
those parts of my magical diary which describe the intense Saturn
Retreat (Saturn Exerzitium, in its original German) that I put myself through in the Spring of 2010. The retreat lasted four weeks and
culminated, on the final day, with my first encounter with my holy
daimon. This particular kind of extended ritual practice is taught as
part of the curriculum of the magical training organization IMBOLC.
This organization was founded in 1992 by Roland Gabler in Kempten,
Germany, as an independent study institute, and it offers an in-depth
magical training for the solitary practitioner in all aspects of Western
hermeticism.[1]

After ten years of active practice and study with IMBOLC, I chose to
conduct this extended ritual retreat as my final piece of work with them
before pursuing my own path. Those four weeks consisted of several magical interventions combined with sleep deprivation, fasting and social isolation. The culmination of the work was the final night when I underwent
the Ritus Thanatos, an experience of being buried alive in the wilderness.

1 Further information, in German, at www.magieausbildung.de

73

The core structure of the Saturn Retreat

- The focus of the first week was to reduce sleep to a minimum. This was done through a sequence of dedicated prayers to Saturn at hourly intervals through the night.
- The focus of the second week was to reduce food consumption to a minimum. This was done through a week-long fast.
- The focus of the third week was to reduce speech to a minimum. This was done through a week spent in silence, or at least speaking no more than was absolutely required.
- The focus of the fourth week was to combine all three reductions: minimal sleep, minimal food, minimal speech.
- In addition, every Saturday, on the morning and evening hours of Saturn, a full ritual of Saturn was performed, and detailed notes and reflections captured in my magical diary.
- On the final night of the fourth week, following the eighth and final Saturn ritual, a ceremonial burial rite was conducted, the Ritus Thanatos.

The diary entries in this part of the book have been translated from German into English. Where additional context is required, I have added it. Some entirely personal matters have been omitted. However, I have made no other changes, so while this record is obviously subjective in nature, it accurately conveys the nature of the ritual experience. I include it in this book for two reasons: firstly, it is a reaction against the West's current fetish for objectivity and secondly, as evidence of my experiences.

Objectivity – the deliberate elimination of every subjective aspect of an experience – has become an unquestioned and seemingly universal standard in every field of research. While objectivity is certainly necessary in, for instance, medicine and some fields of physics, it causes real problems when it is applied to all modes of human enquiry.

Today, 'subjective' is mainly used as a pejorative term which expresses a strong reservation about the reliability of some insight or correlation. It implies some imperfection, some loss of quality, and speaks of phenomena which must remain outside of rational science until they can be reliably replicated and their cause-and-effect patterns established.

Such a perspective rules out a scientific approach to most fields of practical magical enquiry – though there are of course exceptions, such as pragmatic 'folk' and 'success' magic: Did the charm change the weather in time, yes or no? Did the spell bring the lover, yes or no? Did the curse inflict the requested disease, yes or no? Did the prophecy or divination turn out to be true, yes or no? This book, however, is not concerned with that sort of magic.

Not only is the 'raw data' of spirit contact necessarily subjective, but it can no more be replicated than sitting down at the same table in a café every day can be expected to reproduce the same conversation – even with all the same people present. (And of course in real life, and in magic in particular, we are never in a single operator environment.) The essential test for spirit contact is instead whether the information thereby acquired can be applied to the world with positive results. 'Does it work,' not 'can it be objectively scrutinized,' has always been the mantra of the successful magician.

So when you read my magical diary, remember that the content of spirit messages is much less relevant than the methods illustrated for successfully applying that content. Imagine that you are trying to learn to cross rivers by jumping from one stone to another. Memorizing the locations of the stones in any one river is pointless, as every river has different stones. Instead you want to learn what makes for good jumping. How do you alternate movement with stillness? Where are the moments of instability and balance, of relaxation and watchfulness? By publishing some of my subjective experiences, I hope to help you learn, by example, the skill of crossing your own rivers.

Now to my second reason for including part of my diary in this book. Given the subjective nature of our craft, it is imperative for us to provide as much tangible evidence of our work as we can. What have we really done? What have we truly experienced in the circle of the spirits? And how can we demonstrate that we are making reliable observations, drawing reliable conclusions, and avoiding empty claims? The following extracts are intended as evidence of my own path: they illustrate some of the experiences that led to the creation of this book. And as I shall be relying on those experiences when, in the third part of this book, I make suggestions about how you might commune with your holy daimon, it seemed only fair to open this part of my diary to you, so that you could judge my expertise, or lack thereof, for yourself.

It should also be noted that this four week retreat was performed after ten years of active magical practice. For the first five of those years I practised persistently for between one and two hours a day, with almost no exceptions. Our Tibetan relatives seclude themselves for years at a stretch in remote caves to accomplish certain magical processes. The famous Abramelin rite requires eighteen months. There is no shortcut to magical accomplishment. Any solid craft requires persistence, focus, dedication, and humility; and no one easily achieves the spiralling ascent in which one finds oneself shifting constantly between student and teacher. What results a similar four week Saturn Retreat might have for other magicians, I do not know. I know of many magicians whose training ended with a burial rite which did not culminate in communion with their holy daimon – and of course they may not have intended it to. Each of our rivers is different.

Finally, a word on the practical conditions under which this retreat was undertaken. I had just started a new job that required frequent travel, though it also allowed me many days working from home. However, those days had to be spent mainly on the telephone. Taking an extended vacation was therefore not an option, and I kept a somewhat suboptimal silence in the retreat's third week. The retreat was a difficult burden for both me and my wife, and our circumstances at the time did not make it any easier. On the positive side, in 2010 there was no social media to distract me, which made concentrating exclusively on this work somewhat easier than it would be for me today. And we were lucky enough to live out in the relative wilderness, in a 1920s farmhouse. Next to our house were several old barns and a large brick building, covered in ivy, that had been a saddle factory during the Second World War. I had cleaned out this abandoned space and built a large temple area on the ground floor. It was heated by a woodburning stove, and thick black curtains sealed off a spacious square inner temple which contained a handmade altar, banners, and a large magical circle drawn in sanctified chalk on the old wooden floorboards. The wide and empty attic above the ground floor was

accessed by means of an outside staircase which ascended over what had once been a chicken coop, but which now housed mainly spiders, mice, and the occasional weasel. I could not have asked for a better or more romantic environment to perform the many related rituals in – despite the bone-deep cold that left me shivering morning and night once I locked the aged, green door behind me.

＊

From the magical diary of Brother Camaysar, a.k.a. Frater Acher

V.III.MMX · FIRST NIGHT

Tonight, in twenty minutes, my four week Saturn Exerzitium (SatEx) will begin. To the extent that it is possible, I feel reasonably prepared. Today I will spend the first night in the prepared room, interrupting my sleep every hour for brief meditations on Saturn. In memoriam Camaysar. I expect a long march. Patience and sacrifice will be my companion. If a new version of myself is meant to emerge, then the old one first has to yield. Both, old and new selves, however, deserve respect and tolerance. Slow, slow while we walk in Saturn.

VI.III.MMX · FIRST DAY

The getting up every hour of the night was exhausting, as expected. I slept through the hour at 2 a.m. as the alarm did not go off. I awoke again at 3:20 a.m., lit some olibanum incense, and meditated just as in the following hours. Initially it was hard to find an anchor point for my thoughts.

In front of me lay the unveiled talisman and the Zazel egregore, and the image of the Tree of Life hung on the wall before me. A still life. It dawned on me that this would be precisely the journey that I would be on while in SatEx: from the ritualized contact with Saturn, via his dark face called Death and the shadow of excess, to the truthful splendour of Tiphareth. A long path, full of unknown questions and familiar fears.

This morning I initiated the SatEx during the first hour of Saturn with a sixty minute meditation. It seems as if the pressure in my body has slightly increased. Everything seems tighter, yet also somewhat heavier.

Now I am learning by heart the text of the ritual for the first rite, which I shall perform this noon during the second hour of Saturn.

Yesterday night with leads from Agrippa of Nettesheim and the internet I discovered the method to extract the name of my Holy Genius and Evil Demon from my radix. What a coincidence that this happened during the last night before my SatEx dying process.

First Saturn ritual performed. As I needed to stick to the specific hour of Saturn and unfortunately did not have any vacation days leading up

to the SatEx, I was busy with preparations until the last minute. During the initial Lesser Banishing Ritual of the Pentagram (LBRP) I realized how long it had been since I had performed a proper ritual, i.e. worked consciously on the astral plane. Yet as soon as the four angels were present, things improved, and I got access to the current. Good increase of tension following the LBRP and a powerful Hexagram Ritual (HGR). Unfortunately, the prayer and the conjuration I had to read from paper, which reduced my astral consciousness and awareness quite significantly. It is during these moments of the rite, when speaking words learned by heart, that the most powerful forces are set free. The consecration that followed went well; however it took quite a long time for me to perceive Saturn specifically, i.e. subsumable by my astral senses.

It was only at the end of charging the talisman that I suddenly realized the limitless, lifeless vastness beyond the boundary of the magical circle. All life had been confined to something like underground cells in an earth made entirely from ice. Radiating, white snow covered everything, and the sky was starless and filled with deep blackness. Only at the end, when I moved towards the East for the finale LBRP, did I suddenly perceive a presence, an immediate coexistence with me, in the circle. It was not evil; yet it was watchful and completely devoid of any love for life, cold and dry, taking effect in darkness, just like the dissecting knife, a mixture of stone, white snow, and deep night. I left the covered altar prepared for tonight's second ritual.

What a day. Following the second ritual I am completely exhausted (and reeking from incense). If Saturn in the first rite showed me his cold side, tonight he showed me his dark side. I made many small mistakes, especially in the sequencing. In the middle of the ritual I still felt completely alone, as if surrounded by a silent, gaping emptiness. All force and life emitted only from myself. The thought passed through my mind that this may have been because I tried to charge the same talisman twice, so it would not attract the forces anymore as my pledge had already been fulfilled. Maybe that is what it was. Yet towards the end, after fears of failure and loss had seeped into me and I felt crushed by the ritual as if under an immense burden, I realized that this was precisely the dark side of Saturn. Zazel without Agiel. The swamps of sadness. So perhaps the ritual actually worked better than I realized. What remains is my exhaustion, just like after an unacceptably long day. During my meditations tonight I might need to complain to Zazel – and return a few of his thoughts.

After all this I went for a walk with Thor in the afternoon. It was bright sunshine when we left the house. I parked the car and five minutes later a snowstorm engulfed us which lasted for half an hour. When we returned to the car from our walk, the sun smiled on us again. The weather today could not have been more fitting for the SatEx. The previous day it was still so mild, yet today twenty centimetres of new snow. Lo, a beginning.

VII.III.MMX · SECOND DAY

The second night was like the first, except a light headache accompanied me for it. The day had been exhausting and the thick clouds of incense in the temple had been good for Tzaphkiel and the Aralim, but less good for me. I spent the morning cleaning the house for three hours. Unbelievable how much dirt one sees through the eyes of Saturn. The sun is back and the snow is melting again. Just now I see the head of a flower outside around whose petals the snow has already disappeared. It is good to see that Saturn is but one of many forces, and that life knows how to persist.

Tonight during my meditation came the thought: what kind of deaths have I already been dying? Which cuts, that seemed such definite farewells, have I experienced so far in this life? I had to think of my youth, the relationships I had before I met my wife, and the way I had misapplied Saturn towards the end of each one of them and made myself guilty. If I am going to die in four weeks, then how can I forgive myself for this? Or do I simply accept it without redemption?

I still have to clean the temple, create a silk bag for the talisman, and continue the work on the name of my genius.

I finished the work on the name of my genius. A significant, solemn moment, to hold its name in my hands. And suddenly I realize what this work, what the insight of the name of the higher self, has to do with Saturn. Once I am ready to give up myself as an incarnate one, in my mortal shell, then the door will open that leads to the things that lie beyond my birth. And this presence waits, one that outlasts and guides me, one that released me from its arms at my birth and will embrace me again at my death. These things all happen by themselves; they find their own place; only rational deeds can destroy them.

Does the name of the genius outlast my incarnation? Is it a key for which I will search again in my next life? Or is it a continually present expression of time, an arch which spans my possible life and decays with me after it has been lived? Is it a path or a goal? From the eyes of my mortal body it is both, my goal and a path.

The work on the calculation of the name was quite mathematical, structured, factual, and logical, like the pursuit of a hidden and sealed burial chamber. I wonder whether the conjured forces of Saturn were helping me. I can see no other explanation apart from the effects of the ritual contact and the radiating ahead and following echo in time these rites have created. Their effect stretches out in all three dimensions of time, past, present, and future. I am full of gratefulness; something is with me.

VIII.III.MMX · THIRD DAY

The third night was easier than the first two. The getting up, the lighting of the candles, the staring at the Saturn image, it is becoming a ritual. It also helped that I slept nine hours in the last two nights, despite my hourly awakenings, so I gained enough sleep in total. That will definitely change in the coming days and during my trips to Geneva and Milan.

Currently, since yesterday morning it seems I am truly in touch with the bright side of Saturn. I was all by myself during the weekend so didn't have to speak, the house was clean, the outside was covered in snow, and I had time to work on all things Saturnine and magical. For the first time I did not experience any kind of loneliness or fear of being left, but was able to enjoy the silence in quiet contemplation. In between all my jobs, and in all kind of situations, thoughts about death germinated.

IX.III.MMX · FOURTH DAY

Tonight during the meditation the thought: Saturn rules all things of substance. Irrespective of how much I withdraw from it, in the end it will take from me what I love most: my wife. Two thoughts lie buried within this: I dissolve from substance by walking through it in death. And: to dissolve love from substance might be the hardest art of all.

It is 5:30 a.m., and I am almost on my way to Geneva.

X.III.MMX · FIFTH DAY

An interesting observation yesterday: is it the aim of the SatEx to immerse oneself fully in the realm of Saturn and to drown within it? Or is the aim to overcharge oneself deliberately with the forces of Saturn, and so learn to balance them in everyday life? Is it mainly about the experience

of overcharging Saturn, or about one's ability to control the forces of Saturn in even the most extreme circumstances? Should my attitude in this endeavour be mainly an active or a passive one?

The day in Geneva yesterday brought Saturn back into its balance with the other planetary forces, particularly Mercury and Jupiter. Nevertheless, the focus on Saturn was present with me all the time. For the first time in the last five days I experienced Saturn as one force among seven equals, and not as the dominant, tall, black figure made of shadows. Its effect, once considered as one of seven integral components, is entirely different: it's a force that structures, clarifies, and that maintains a distance. Simultaneously I felt how uncomfortable it was for my Saturn-saturated presence to grant the other six forces their own rightful space.

A second point: In the invocation I turn to all mediating agents of Saturn: the planet, the divine name, choirs of angels, archangel, intelligence, and demon. My assumption is that this has an inherently balancing and positive impact on the full spectrum of Saturnine forces. A conjuration of Tzaphkiel or Zazel by themselves would most likely yield altogether different results. Saturn is an entire world with forces in itself, a planet, as the name says. One just needs to consider the differentiation we see in the forces of our own planet, Earth. We speak of the sublunary forces, and those of the four elements in particular. Saturn knows a similar diversity – or more specifically, below its moons. A significant job within the SatEx is therefore to maintain the various Saturnine forces in balance. No excess in Zazel, no lack of functioning of the Aralim. Only once one has passed in such manner through the gate of Saturn does one gain access to its sublunary atmosphere where one can begin to explore the various force-fields in particular.

The hours between 3 a.m. and 5 a.m. are the most exhausting ones of the night. I started using the six sacred names as a mantra over the Saturn talisman. Tonight this induced Saturnine dreams: tomorrow night I shall check if this was a coincidence.

Rose is back from Berlin.

XI.III.MMX · SIXTH DAY

Exhausting night. The day in Geneva and the work until 9 p.m. yesterday required a lot of energy. Tonight I missed the hourly awakening twice due to tiredness. Also yesterday evening Rose wasn't doing well, and I was doubting the SatEx and the additional strain it will put on our relationship for now and for the three weeks to come.

On the way home from Mailand it clicked. I read several blogs in which grimoire magicians from the USA shared their experiences with the spirits. And suddenly my grasp of the whole thing opened up like a door.

84

So much of my previous magic will become obsolete, even distracting, in the future. I had been present with the spirits, but I had never opened my eyes. They are all here, a living, sleeping, acting reality. The aim of ritual trance is not only the experience of the daimonic current, inarticulate and all-perceiving as it is, but also dialogue with it. They are here, have always been here, ready to participate, to talk and partake. All I have to do is to pull out a chair for them and offer them a seat at the table.

While thinking this through it also clicked, regarding the SatEx, that Acher is withdrawing into himself, even retreating into death, to make space in life and spirit for someone else. This is a radical change, a turning away from the Malkuth that is without spiritual life, and an entrance into the Malkuth that is full of the forces of the magical realm. Only now do I see a vision of the goal of my search.

XII.III.MMX · SEVENTH DAY

Following the lines from yesterday and the day in Mailand I was completely exhausted. I got up once again to meditate at 1 am, then I slept through until 5 am, completely exhausted. That's why today I felt more replenished than all last week. As I said: the more I seem to wane as an incarnated person, the more my magical higher self seems to gain in agency and shine through me. Do I have to exhaust and starve out the veil of Malkuth to see through it? Tomorrow is the second Saturday: two further Saturn rites are awaiting me, as well as the beginning of the fast.

XIII.III.MMX · EIGHTH DAY

The first night in my own bed next to Rose made a huge difference. How easily good sleep pulls one back from imbalance. Instead today was the first day without food. It is now 7:45 p.m. and I cannot recall ever not having eaten for such a long time. It is not even unpleasant. I only hope my stomach remains this stoic.

I am sure the difference between the first and the second week will be obvious. Withdrawal of sleep and induction of hunger in their own way both create space for the forces of Saturn. The rite of Saturn today cannot be compared to those of last week: the talisman had already been charged, I used my magical mirror to speak to Saturn directly. Furthermore, I did not wear my old lamen. It was inscribed with the name of Camaysar and it's not fitting for Acher any longer. These were the answers to the questions I asked in the rite:

What can I learn from you?
The black art.
On what matters can I enquire of you?

I cleanse life through death.
Shall I call you in ritual or in meditation?
I am here, all the time.
In what circumstances do you bring death?
When the blood is saturated.
What can I do for you?
Lend me your senses (mouth and eye).

After the final question I felt Saturn flowing into me, filling and saturating my whole being. It was black and at the same time bright white; it was totally clear and completely undiluted. I asked one final question:

How can you help me strengthen my magic?
By making you stronger.

Just like last week, I realize there is a Day-Saturn and a Night-Saturn. The one during the day clarifies and provides structure; the one during the night is dark, fear inducing, threshold-like.

In terms of procedure, the second ritual was good, yet my magic had already been drained and was significantly lower. The sphere of the elements was clear and enclosed, and the sphere of Saturn within was made strong and stable. It turns out to make a huge difference if my spoken words are actually addressed to another being, if I speak to an actual conscious, living force – and if my voice is not acting only as a tool to build up rhythm and vibration in space. Again, I had questions for Saturn:

What is the black art?
To turn ♄ *(lead) into* ☉ *(gold).*
To which kind of knowledge are you the gate?
To life I am the gate.
What is it that humans can do to prevent your pain?
Humility, modesty, and having a goal.
Why did I suffer so much under you as a child?
An alchemical process, a transformation of soul.
What is my function today in your realm?
To teach how to solve and how to bind.
What can I do for you?
Carry me into life.

After completing the rite the last question still echoed in me. Suddenly I saw a heavily disabled child in front of me. I was shocked, in emotional upheaval provoked by the analogy of the image, and I needed to concentrate completely on the closing act of banishing. Then I realized: a crippled child is the crippled Saturn brought to life, or maybe a metaphorical image expressing this idea. I would have to ask him in the next rite what could lead to such disfigurement, and how it could be prevented.

XIV.III.MMX · NINTH DAY

The fast is taking energy, it starves my body. My legs feel as if I had come in from a long run: their muscles ache. The walks with Thor are exhausting. In addition, they are beginning to affect my mood and I realize how irritable I have become. Possibly I shall have to change to dry bread and soup when I am in England next week.

I began reading the *Arbatel*. Based on it I will be able to build my own path into evocation magic, beginning with the Olympic spirits. I believe my time with IMBOLC has come to an end. From here on I have to train myself if I truly aspire to walk a mystical path. There is no longer any reason to wait.

I just finished a Saturn meditation and spirit journey. Behind the door of Saturn there was a labyrinth of black metal mines. They were crystalline in shape and deeply jagged. Bottomless pits fell off in all directions, the rock was cold, black, and metallic, and there was no path to walk. I jumped across one of the pits and balanced on the ledge behind it. There was no advancing; the atmosphere did not let me fly either. I called for Tzaphkiel. Nothing happened. Then I jumped back to the place where I had come from, and turned around. Suddenly a white, radiating angel hung in the air, holding a spear or a scythe in its hand. It did not reply to my questions, did not provide its name, and something seemed deceitful and malicious about it. I pushed it away with my dagger and it disappeared into the shaft behind it. Through the sign of Saturn I leapt back to where my body was waiting for me.

Saturn is no country for vacations.

XV.III.MMX · TENTH DAY

Because of my strict fast, I have lost three kilograms in only two days. I have begun to feel a slight pain in my heart. It seems my metabolism is still working too fast. I started today to take a little liquid nutrition: a processed muesli and a carrot and ginger soup. A lot of energy returned immediately. Even though I felt weak, I could work with focus from 8 am until 9 p.m., interrupted only by two walks with Thor.

XVI.III.MMX · ELEVENTH DAY

This morning I did a forty-five minute Saturn meditation, just as on Sunday. As part of this I change my entire body, through and through, into black stone which I pull down from the sphere of Saturn. For the first time today I felt the power and might of the planet as I approached it in vision. It is made of the toughest dead rock and so are its shadowy rings. Saturn is a guardian of borders who keeps his silence and never alters his goal until the assignment is accomplished or it makes him perish in the process. His silence is threatening and yet a foundation on which anything can be built.

When I took up the SatEx, my expectation was that it would basically cut out anything dead from my life and that it would overhaul my every-day world. But I had already let go so many old and used-up things over the course of the last eighteen months. London, my old job, my tendency to overburden, my habit of contemplating which is futile in itself, the tension between boy and man, all this ended in 2009. What I did not expect was the sweeping effect that it would have on my magic. Here evo-cation magic, angelic magic, contact with my holy guardian angel and new techniques are all stepping right into my life, and overthrowing long-re-spected and deeply familiar beliefs and rituals. Welcome! I have waited so long for this, I have been so busy having taken so long approaching it that walking was all that I had in my view and my actual goal had disappeared from sight. It feels so right and healthy to take this new path, this new beginning.

XVII.III.MMX · TWELFTH DAY

This day has been atypical, and the next two will be likewise. I am north of Oxford at our regional company meeting. I can't live on buttermilk and juices, and am surrounded all day by many people. Saturn doesn't like this at all. It will be hard to reestablish balance; I will meditate in the morn-ing and at night, and will reduce my nutrition, even though I must also eat solid food here, though an absolute minimum of it. It goes to show

how little space we have in our everyday work lives for Saturn. Quite the opposite. Everything has its time, and it is quite hard to live as a hermit for even four weeks. It is much more like the coming and going of waves which unknowingly pull one further out to sea. A sea full of Saturn, full of cold, black stone.

We managed to book a really run-down hotel in the countryside, much to the dismay of everyone else, but to my pleasure. The food is bad and scant and the rooms are old and unkempt. Concentration, reduction, letting go, preventing, giving in. Being silent to be able to speak again.

An interesting thought in the book by Stephen Flowers yesterday: when faced with suffering or problems, and equally when especially happy, attempting to further increase light and love resembles the man who, standing on train tracks, covers his eyes with his hands and refuses to step off them. Only the path into darkness, into loneliness, the acknowledgement of silence and reflection, even death and letting die, is to step off the tracks. Life does not create such a balance by itself. We do. It's our free will that decides.

XVIII.III.MMX · THIRTEENTH DAY

This day just passed by so quickly. I had to give an important presentation; the Saturnine aspects of concentration, structure, clarity, and logic came in handy. Towards the end of the day NN spoke to us in quite a moving way. It took a while for the spark to catch me. Then I suddenly realized that it was precisely this warmth of heart which I had abandoned over the previous days, and for which I tend to live so much on all other days. It is unbelievable the drastic changes we can induce within ourselves before we ever begin to notice them. A change of paradigm is the best example: adapting to the new normal with unbelievable speed, integrating it, embracing it, until we no longer even recognize it as something foreign. And possibly it has stopped being foreign. The true loss in such a moment, however, is the one over the certainty of what is truly of oneself. If anything foreign can become innate, then what really differentiates myself? If *Sondersein* (being different) is no longer possible, and yet no gnostic unity dawns beyond it, then I am losing myself in multiplicity, in fragmentation. Loss of identity.

XX.III.MMX · FIFTEENTH DAY

Third Saturday, first Saturn ritual. Despite my rushed preparations, successful. Already right after the Hexagram ritual I could feel the vibrations of the name IHVH Elohim. It was a mosaic made up of a structure of radiating white triangles that filled, vibrating and yet incredibly stable, the entire magical circle. At this point I had not yet intoned any of the other

names of Saturn. I realized in this moment how significantly diverse the various aspects of Saturn's being are as identified by its many names. It is an entirely unique microcosm within them, and the ritual structure of the Golden Dawn is just aiming at a mean average, i.e. the simultaneous vibration of all its influences. Under such circumstances the targeted contact with e.g. Tzaphkiel is impossible; however, it allows the meta or hive being of Saturn a direct interaction with me, and vice versa. I have never before encountered these different octaves with such rich textures.

During the peak of the rite, Saturn took the whole magical sphere and filled it completely with clear black stone. It penetrated me, my body, grew through me, and still let me move within it. Here are the answers to my questions:

How can you assist me in a full astral journey?
Do not look for a border, look for a gate. The black mirror.
Which border is marked by your planet Shabbathai?
The border of life sustaining structures. The border of Zimzum.
What is the nature of Aratron?
The stone engraving chisel. Metal.
What is the nature of Tzaphkiel?
The pillar of ascent. The black canal.
What is the function of the Aralim?
The black circle bounding life. They herd all living things like sheep. They are the circular mirror, enclosed in itself, and reflecting all influences of life upon one another.

As it replied to the last question, I saw a closed circle of black-feathered angels with red eyes all around me. They stood in complete silence, like a living wall or chain of darkness that concentrated all life and light in itself. The outer skin of creation.

Even though the last few days in England have not been as strict as the previous ones, I still feel exhausted. On the one hand this is due to work itself, on the other it is due to the mental and spiritual effort of the SatEx. It seems as if I am dragging myself up a ladder, holding on to my own head. Unforgiving, estranged from life in order to transcend life. I wonder if there is a parallel path that goes through love? Or is this the path of ascesis and therefore always the path of austerity from all things beloved?

I am putting Rose and myself through a hard test. Saturn radiates even upon her.

XXI.III.MMX · SIXTEENTH DAY
The second Saturn ritual, just as with the previous Saturday, was of a different character. The presence, nearness, and density of the morning ritual was replaced by a black, empty, cold void. At some point the five hexagrams seemed like the silver bars of a cage beyond which the infinite extent of emptiness spreads itself out. Here are the answers to my questions to Saturn:

How should I make use of the black mirror?
A black ocean, a current through the mirror. Swim.
For which functions can I enquire of Aratron?
The duration within time and within the body. Works of preservation and destruction.
For which functions can I enquire Tzaphkiel?
The ascending and descending. Works of motion within time and across the planes.
What is causing miscarriages?
(white silver demons against a black background)
What is causing disabled children?
Particular circumstances and requirements for particular alchemical (soul) processes.
What can man do to preserve health through you?
Avoid poisons, live in purity, do not spoil things, allow the alchemical processes to take place without interference.

Saturn increasingly seems to me like the guardian overseeing each individual's predetermined developmental processes. It is the sealed athanor, the goal of the alchemist which takes time and yet aims to transcend all cyclical changes through time. It is the concentration on each phase of the work, so that the whole work might succeed. While engaged in this work, Saturn is entirely without mercy, just like the alchemist is without mercy to the ashes, the fire, and the metals. His laws are boundaries, dosages, insulation, conjunction, and patience. And it is a fickle and blind man who crosses Saturn's path. That's why the coercion, that's why all the awful suffering. We are amidst the fire. We simmer, evaporate, burn, blaze, blacken and fall to ashes.

What roles do the other planets play in this process? If Saturn is the guardian of the alchemical stages of life, then what functions do the other planets have?

XXIV.III.MMX · NINETEENTH DAY

The last two days passed without any special events. My periods of silence are short and therefore not especially hard, as I cannot avoid talking while working. Abstinence from all media, sugar, and coffee is harder. Just as in previous weeks, I take any opportunity to relax or recharge unconsciously and purely by use of sensual stimuli.

I sense a huge tiredness within me; on the one hand it is purely from the exhausting last two-and-a-half weeks; on the other hand it is also tiredness from the energies of Saturn itself. The lack of Moon, Venus, Jupiter – and especially the Sun. The tiredness of being a prisoner within oneself and the exhaustion of the ascetic.

Two days ago I had an interesting dream. Through a kind of grey mist, I walked into the astral realm. There I was haunted by black shadows in the shape of humans. It seemed like a training camp, where my job was to channel names, to grasp them mentally as they were given to me by the shadows. Then I was in a foreign medieval town. An old man, gaunt but strong, lived in a church with a large mechanical instrument that was buried deep underground. It seemed like a mechanical-alchemical process maintained by use of fire, smoke, steam, and swinging wheels, all underground. Everything was spinning and hissing like a huge piece of clockwork, and the old man was jumping from a lever to the fire to a bucket of water and pushing the whole thing steadily further. He permitted me to stand in the entrance to his cellar; he somehow even seemed proud to be watched as he conducted his meticulous work; yet he did not show any emotions, but was entirely concentrated on his work.

The old man is Saturn itself. The church is a metaphor for the living current beginning to fill my faith and magical work. But how in the long haul can I keep this living clockwork in motion, deep beneath the foundations of my church?

XXVI.III.MMX · TWENTY-FIRST DAY
Tonight I went to the gym and encountered the white and black Saturn. The black: the witch Saruya suddenly appeared with her daughter and granddaughter in the doorway. Almost ten years ago I visited her in her shop in Munich. Back then she made a real impression on me, almost a personification of the 'real' magical life. Today she seemed more like a failed attempt to personify Saturn. Haggard, sunken, labouring after beauty and yet radiating sternness through and through. Her granddaughter, who I remember having seen lodged in the dark back of the shop like a piece of furniture, must now be eight or nine years old. She was completely overwrought, as if suffering from the lack of exchange and contact at

home, in the house in which Saturn lives. I have to add here that when I met Saruya in her shop, she told me she was preparing incense for remote killings for some of her more special clients. I remember her large, white hands, strong as a man's. She probably just wanted to impress me. Yet I have come to remember her as pure, black Saturn.

The white Saturn: In the dressing room I suddenly found myself before an old, white-haired man whom I had already seen in the gym area. He had been doing each exercise extremely slowly, with incredible concentration and steadiness. He asked me if I would come back tomorrow and I declined, saying that once a week was enough for me. He shook his head, smiling, and said that I had to come at least two or three times per week. Then he told me that he was seventy-four years and had been training in this place for at least ten years now. That was the only reason, according to him, that he had stayed so fit and didn't suffer from his age as much as his sisters did. He had a cataract and could no longer hear well – hearing and vision were failing him – but other than that he was perfectly healthy thanks to his discipline, perseverance, and training. He kept on smiling all the while, and seemed to be amused by his own smartness or just about the simplicity of a good life.

The SatEx works like a rock thrown into the sea. I am the rock. In exchange for giving up my ability to breathe, I get to make wonderful discoveries on the ocean floor. But this ocean is made entirely of rock, and there is no up or down. Not my body alone, but my entire self, the entire human being, is what forms the athanor. I am the flask – body, spirit, and soul – for the Higher Brother and his influence through the prism of the seven rays. The SatEx teaches me not to intervene, not to disturb the processes, to be subdued and silent, and to give up all thoughts that emerge from the place called 'I.'

Two nights ago I had a dream. I had been captured and someone had injected a yellow, viscous liquid into my blood. The yellow substance wanted to mix with my blood, and it was able to enter or leave my body through all my orifices. It was this liquid that makes humans moaning, suffering, lethargic, and inert. It was this substance that keeps humans trapped within themselves. My torturers made fun of me as I grew weaker and weaker. Then, suddenly, I chopped off my whole arm, and in a single stroke cleared my whole body of the liquid. Suddenly I was unbound, strong, and free. I ran and escaped from my torturers, floating upwards from the town into the night. I awoke and had the following sentence or insight in my mind: 'Alchemy is what resides behind the Magic.'

XXVII.III.MMX · TWENTY-SECOND DAY

The first Saturn ritual on this fourth Saturday was weaker than some of the previous ones. I was exhausted just as before, and didn't give myself enough time to prepare. Still, I was in contact with Saturn and received answers to my questions:

What is the raw substance of the alchemical process called life?
Blood fertilized by light.
What is the aim of this alchemical process called life?
Experience, feathers, ascent, Solve.
How can I support this process through magic?
A blade. Separating.
Which function does Shabbathai have in this process?
To uphold the boundaries of life; to bound the place of creation.
Which function does Shemesh have in this process?
Impetus; to create the tension of life.
Which function does Levanah have in this process?
Connecting; the rhythmical equalization of forces.
Reveal to me the current alchemical process within myself?
To create ashes for new life.
What do I have to do to communicate with my Holy Angel?
Trumpet, trombone. To call for it.
What can I do for you?
Lend me your senses.

After the last answer, clear, clashing ice rushed through me and filled the whole magical circle. It seems to me that I lost a lot of energy in this moment.

When I got to the end of the ritual, I was completely exhausted. I thought of the end of the SatEx, felt like a stone underwater, being crushed by the weight of Saturn.

The rest of the day I spent crafting a Saturn lamen. It came out as I wanted it: a heavy and black plate of metal with black chains. Its front and cover have the two sides of my Saturn pentacle. It should help with the vision in the mirror and work as a bridge to close the magical circuit. It will

certainly require charging energy. I really should charge it from the energy of the ritual circle and not take further energy from my own organism.

The second Saturn ritual was the strongest so far. I went into the temple an hour early, lit the fire, sat down in front of it, stared into the flames, and meditated. The ritual took exactly an hour. It helped me clarify a lot.

First the answers:

What is the goal of the process called life?
(no answer)
How can I produce blood fertilized by light?
Lightning that strikes into water.
Of which nature is the angel Hocroel?
(no answer, then:) *Dragon. Red.*
What is the learning goal of next week for me?
(I see a black cross on a coffin. There is life surrounding the coffin.)
What can I do to support this process?
To withdraw from all sensual impressions.
Should I perform the finishing rite of the SatEx in the forest or here?
In the forest. Through the dark into fear.
Which advice do you have for me for the time afterwards?
A tight belt. Strictness and deprivation uphold contact.

I had already realized earlier that each name of Saturn (IHVH Elohim - Tzaphkiel - Aralim - Shabbathai - Agiel - Zazel) brings an entirely unique dynamic and motion into the magical circle:

· IHVH Elohim creates the magical circle of Saturn.
· Tzaphkiel is a middle pillar of energy;
· Aralim are a choir of black angels surrounding the circle;
· Shabbathai fills the sphere of Saturn with substance;
· Agiel's impact is centripetal.

In their entirety, these forces come together like living clockwork, a key that unlocks the forces of Saturn. At the same time the banner seems to have a kind of shielding function.

My thoughts were more focused and precise during this ritual. My questions on the details of the alchemical process, however, were not relevant. Saturn is just one component in the entire process, thus it could not answer the question regarding the goal of the process called life. Furthermore, my consciousness couldn't lend Saturn the right vocabulary, as my untrained mind could only express itself in crude images. If only I knew more about this kind of alchemy, if only I knew the exact vocabulary, then Saturn could provide me with precise answers.

The answer to the sixth question opened my eyes. Saturn's advice doesn't need to be to the same as my own. He wants me to bury myself in the forest and pass through the terror and fear that follows. In this case the extremity and intensity of the death rite would come to the fore. The alternative is to construct a coffin right above the temple, in the old empty attic of the barn, and be confined there. Here the analogy of dying on a 'higher plane' (and being born again) is front and centre. Here I turn myself into the golem of my higher guardian angel and destroy my ego. In the forest, fear and the destruction of my physical body and ego is the focus; in the attic, gaining a new stability beyond the grave is the focus.

XXVIII.III.MMX · TWENTY-THIRD DAY

Yesterday night, after the second rite and throughout the night, I was exhausted. The remaining five days will be a tug of war with my willpower. It is not even that I am physically drained or exhausted; quite the opposite. Rarely have I ever felt as healthy and strong (even if not vital) as I do right now. Saturn seems to be a paradox: on the one hand it grants health for as long as one subdues oneself to its strict discipline. On the other hand it brings death when the time is ripe.

Moments of deep magical insight and progress mix with moments of complete despondency. I could also say: whenever I live Saturn, I am charged with concentration and perseverance. As soon as I dip my toe into any of the other of the seven planetary realms, the floor crumbles beneath my feet.

I spent most of the day today creating Trithemius's Table of Practice for crystal visions. As I need all the planetary and archangelic kameas, I will continue to create these on the computer tomorrow. On Tuesday I will be able to put the mirror into service on its new throne in the temple. I am interested to learn what will happen if I conjure e.g. Tzaphkiel outside of a full rite, but as part of a meditation, into the black mirror. It would be such a practical relief to take up the contact outside of a ritual, and possibly even in a stable manner.

XXIX.III.MMX · TWENTY-FOURTH DAY

Tonight, Rose and I argued. She asked why I was doing this to us. I said because I had already welched on too many of Saturn's tests in my life. It tore my heart out to say it. I am so far removed from normal life, from love, happiness, and togetherness. And still I know, this exercise, this boundary violation, is what takes the wind out of death's sails. For now.

Why am I doing this to her? Normally such pain is accepted only under duress, and at times of insoluble paradox, and even then one does not stop trying to understand why. Perhaps it is ultimately about separating the experience of pain from the experience of harm so that Saturn need not harm me to enter my life. Because enter it shall, according to the rule of life. Saturn's chalice passes by no one. However, precisely because of the SatEx I get to taste its bitterness, I get to have the experience of bitterness without swallowing the actual poison. Undoubtedly this is a paradox not to be understood by anyone who does not walk an occult path.

And it is true: Saturn is bitter, without a doubt. Yet instead of his harmful side, I am beginning to discover the healing side of Saturn. This side of Saturn is so rarely observed because normally, when he appears on one's doorstep, one immediately slams the door on him; he has to find his way in through the chimney, or through people's bodies. His healing side is unruly, strict, uniform, cold. But it is rich in insights, full of secrets, and full of things well hidden from the hands of life.

Today I almost completed the Table of Practice. Only the final printed seal is still missing. The summary of all the seals of the planetary angels was much more time consuming than expected. Also I purchased all the components of my coffin. Tomorrow I will paint the wood and screw it

together. It is time for this to end. My willpower is running dry. I feel like an animal who has forgotten the path to its watering hole. If we were rider and mount, then I would have climbed off days ago and started walking next to my donkey. Be brave now.

XXX.III.MMX · TWENTY-FIFTH DAY

I barely slept this night. It was a full moon and thoughts of the construc-
tion of my coffin kept me awake. After all, how often in life does one
get to construct the place of one's death? But the coffin is more than a
place; much more. It is the symbol for the territory that I have traversed
in the SatEx. Creating it was like a glance into the valley, having already
climbed the nearby steep mountain. So much will I have to leave behind
in it. Some of it I know already; much hasn't even begun to dawn on me.
Not knowing whom I will be in ten months, triggered by these weeks, by
this approaching moment. More precisely: it is the glance into the valley,
before one jumps off the mountain.

Despite the terrible night, I worked for twelve hours straight without
a single break. First I had to finish the Table of Practice, then clean the
house, and finally I began work on the coffin. It is done now and rests,
waiting, in the large empty attic above the temple. I am going to be the
golem of my angel; my spirit with it, my body here on earth. I am the
root, and it is the light above my crown.

Still three days to go.

XXXI.III.MMX · TWENTY-SIXTH DAY

Yesterday, in the gym sauna, I suddenly realized the meaning of the magical sacrifice. And now I seem to understand the whole meaning of the
SatEx. It was so close all along.

I wrote in the beginning that the SatEx is both a turning away from and
an entering into Malkuth. In reality, however, it is a passage. That is what
Saturn meant when he said my current alchemical process was creating
'ashes for new life.' That is the function of the sacrifice, and the meaning
of the ascetic purification process of the sacrifice itself in advance of its
offering: to prepare the cleanest, purest, most unspoiled ashes for a new
life. The creation of this new substance, from the ashes, that is what it is
all about.

Here is a straightforward example. When people eat the Easter lamb,
the power of the lamb is not converging with them. But in their stomachs
the lamb is losing its form (Saturn) and being burned to ashes. It is these
ashes that are the carrier, the mediating substance, of a much higher force

– the force to which it was consecrated. That is how direct contact with the divine is made possible: by producing the divine substance within our own bodies. And when I lay down as a sacrifice in the coffin, it is nothing else; as a sacrifice I offer my bodily form, and my emotional and mental gestalt. Over four long weeks I have purified them and prepared them for this moment. Yet the asceticism was no end, but merely an alchemical condition. In the passage of the sacrifice, in the moment of losing my shape and becoming ashes, I shall pass over the threshold of Saturn. That is why he is misunderstood as terrifying: because he cannot allow anything over his threshold that still holds a form. He needs the demonic agency – the sleeping on the ground, the hunger, the exhaustion, the tiredness, the single-mindedness and yes, the fear – to raise the energy and force it takes to shed all forms. Only then may we cross over his threshold, and on the other side, discover truly new things.

However, all these new things are connected directly to abilities that we already have, yet today they are tarnished and cloaked, made invisible by the veil of Malkuth. The force that grasps the ashes of the lamb, that begins to dwell in it and saturate it, is an analogue of the spirit of the original lamb, but of an entirely different plane. Only then does Kether arrive in Malkuth. So today I am an analogue of what I will become, and even what I will ever be capable of becoming. But in my current form I am holding back these forces and do not let them through. I have to shed all form (the 'I') to initiate the embodiment of the other possibilities (the 'Self'). That is the meaning of magical sacrifice. And that is the goal of the SatEx, a goal no one has ever described to me in such a fashion. That is why the burial rite in the attic seemed so much more fitting, and the idea of turning myself into the golem of my angel. Maybe this is where the Book of Clay finds its full meaning?

So many insights, so many revelations. But at what price? I had always thought that once we live a happy, ungrudging, fulfilled life, we get to experience the happiness of God. It seems I was naive to want both a perfected and a formless love at the same time.

If I have to let go of everything and turn my back on life just to be this close to the angels, then I know what I will choose. I love my life wholeheartedly; I love Rose, at once so close and so far from me; I love our togetherness, our adventures, our lust for life, our house, our dog, our going to bed, our evenings, our mornings. What could ever beat this? My life, my love with Rose is priceless. I separated myself from her for four weeks. Not a day longer.

I came closer than ever before in my life to death, to pain, to loneliness, to the forces of Saturn, and to the voices of the angels. But nothing can compare to my life, or could be better than it. If I am to become the golem of my angel, then I just hope my angel will love my life as much as I do. Together we can travel and be victorious on our further magical adventures, just like this one. But if it cannot love this life, right here and right now, then we will see each other but once again, upon my death, when I must return to Saturn and the black Aralim one last time.

Yet deep inside myself I know: this is but the experience of a single path. This is not the only door to the house of the angels. (...)

I.IV.MMX · TWENTY-SEVENTH DAY

The image of becoming the golem of my angel doesn't quite hit the nail on the head. Certainly many parts of my life and personality will need to become mutable and somewhat formless, like clay, so that my angel and I can bring each other into alignment.

Rose and I recently talked a lot about how many of our single friends had become so 'whole' in their singleness that it was hard for anyone else to find an opening into their perfectly orchestrated lives. This is precisely how it is with the contact with the angel – and Saturn is the moment as well as the tool of breaking myself open. This was the idea that led me to the image of the golem.

The symbol of the seventeenth path, however, is the twins. Despite being attuned, we will still remain two separate beings, both alive and full of individuality. Gareth Knight uses the metaphor of Castor and Pollux, two brothers of the same mother, yet one of human descent (Castor/Malkuth) and the other divine (Pollux/Binah). Pollux, the half-divine one, decides to spend half his life in hell to rescue his brother Pollux. What a terrific image to illustrate the humility and the 'downwards-directed meditation' of our angel. Impressed by the love of the brothers, Zeus turns them into a twin star in the heavens. The Lovers is the trump of the seventeenth

path: in the image of Castor and Pollux we see the love between the higher and lower mirror images of the same divine spark.

The answer to my question, though, lies neither in Binah nor in Saturn, but in Tiphareth. Thanks to Gareth Knight's wonderful explanation, I am now realizing what has to become of the ashes: it is Tiphareth itself.

(...)

II.IV.MMX · TWENTY-EIGHTH DAY (*final day*)

Let us bring this to completion. Outside, dusk is settling and the last day of the SatEx is coming to an end.

The last four weeks have been a long march through a dark tunnel. The tunnel of single-mindedness, of complete devotion to Saturn, and the darkness of asceticism. How many things have I lost? What did Saturn consider dead and make fall away? It is still much too early to say.

What I know since yesterday, though, is that I walked through this tunnel backwards, with my back to the light at the far end. As soon as I turn around, the sun will shine again on my face. It is good to know what I want to maintain from these weeks and which character traits I shall be giving up for good tonight.

What will follow from this work is not entirely clear yet. First I must reestablish the balance of my energies. My throat chakra is completely overcharged and my heart chakra is dead silent, like an empty house. Then to create a talisman for my angel in Tiphareth. It will help me remain in touch with Pollux and strengthen and grow my magical intent. Thirdly, to leave IMBOLC and to hand over the place of the guide to my angel and myself. An important step to begin forging my own path. And finally, to possibly work through the *Arbatel* in 2010 and 2011 as my first practical grimoire and to gain familiarity with the Olympic spirits and the method of evocation. I actually had the thought that I could work on this last point together with NN. That would be quite a nice celebration of our brotherhood in magic.

And here is the list of the things that will be dying tonight:

- I will move from a perspective of ego towards a perspective of you.
- I will move from the foolishness of the child to the smile of a man.
- I will move from relaxation by overloading my senses to relaxation by offloading my senses.
- I will move into speaking only half of everything I say to everything I say.
- I will move into understanding words as talismans.
- I will move from the consciousness in Malkuth towards a consciousness in Tiphareth.
- I will move from I to Thou.

One more hour until the ritual preparations begin. I am nervous and I am afraid. This is how someone must feel who is about to enter the operating room for some long-awaited yet still dreaded surgery.

III.IV.MMX

Yesterday night, around 10 p.m., I started with the temple preparations. I returned to the house at about 2 a.m.

I was in a strange mood, somewhere between expectation and fear, certainty and uncertainty. One the one hand I was beginning to see my life after the SatEx increasingly clearly, and on the other hand I was full of expectations of death and thoughts of conclusion.

The ninth Saturn ritual went well. Overall it was somewhat shorter than the previous ones. Initially I lacked concentration, probably because of that strange mix of excitement, tiredness, and exhaustion. Several times I had to bring myself back into ritual trance by intoning the divine names. At the peak of the rite I had a vivid understanding of Saturn as the Ur-father as well as in the shape of his angelic forces. My plea was understood and accepted.

Then I asked Saturn for advice about the time that would follow this night. He gave me the four letters H-E-V-D, which I yet have to analyse and understand.

Following the rite I changed my clothes, put on the new robe, and with candle in hand left the temple, walked through the cold night and up the old staircase behind the barn, into the attic for the Ritus Thanatos.

I lit some Saturn incense behind the talisman of Agiel and Zazel and sat down in a triangle of candles in the middle of which stood the coffin.

Staring at the coffin I meditated on death and immersed myself entirely into the perspective of my dying self. This moment was about a farewell without a return, about the decay inside the house of the coffin, about my farewell to Rose, to all the things unfinished as well as about the sadness of everyone left behind.

I extinguished the candles and placed myself in the coffin.

It was a cold night. As I blew out the candles I saw the silver clouds of my breath, and a cold draught blew through the air holes at the top and bottom of the coffin. Only now, in the complete, pitch black darkness of

the coffin, did I once again feel my tiredness and exhaustion. Coldness and stiffness crept into my body and I took up the visualization of death and the decay of my body.

At an early stage I had a clear vision of a radiating and pulsating silver spiral, in whose centre was my dead body. The spiral seemed alive, and something inside it – or maybe the lights it consisted of – began to work on me. Again and again the images of the vision blurred. It certainly wasn't a linear process, more a slow flood made of individual waves, each one pulling me further away from life.

Finally I lay completely reduced to bones in the coffin, dead, half-naked, half covered by the decaying scraps of what once had been my clothes. At this point I was completely without fear. I tested myself several times, to see if I had withheld or suppressed fears. But neither seemed to be the case. Even when my flesh was falling apart, and heaps of maggots piled up in my stomach, my sex and legs, it still seemed like a completely organic and appropriate process.

At a certain point, entirely by itself, my skeleton fell apart into ashes.
Then a particular process set in whose vision I followed with complete
surprise and without any interference on my part. Things happened quite
quickly: the ashes were lifted up (or did they rise aloft themselves?) and
were sifted through a fine screen. Rough, white residue was caught on the
screen and left behind. Then the finer, sifted ashes were picked up again
and poured into a phial in which they were washed. The residue of this
washing was then heated, the fluid began to sweat, and it evaporated and
condensed at the upper end of the glass flask. The drops trickled down
the glass and into another vessel – or perhaps back into the coffin – and
settled down into a human form made entirely of the purified material.
The substance seemed like a firm powder, somewhere between silver and
sand, and between grey and white in colour, and it was quietly radiating.

Without warning I was pushed back into this body – changed from im-
movable spectator into participant – having 'become' this form of ashes.
It seemed as if my spirit had waited outside while the substance of my life
was processed and refined, and then with one big pull I was back, in the
form of these ashes. It felt slightly cold, and yet I was incredibly alive and
brimming with energy.

I had almost no time to experience this before thousands of small,
colourful flower buds broke through the grey surface of the ashes. In a
heartbeat their little heads covered my whole body, without leaving a
single inch clear. I could now sense that my feet, legs, stomach, chest, and
especially my featureless face were all made of these tiny, bright blossoms.
The feeling was completely inexpressible: firm and light at the same time,
stable and agile, fluid and yet solid. My insides were still made entirely of
the strange, grey, ash-like substance, only its whole surface was covered in
thousands, maybe millions, of blossoms.

I expected this to be the highly fulfilling end of the vision. My breath
was calm and steady, and pure energy was flowing into and out of me.
Then from out of nowhere something like a tube pierced my solar plexus.
Through it a current of pure, fluid gold poured into my body. The gold –
or a brightly shining substance that seemed to be gold – began to fill the
grey bodily substance underneath the skin of petals. Only then did I recognize a tall, silver-black figure standing at the head of the coffin. From

out of itself – or did it hold it in its hands? – it threw down a second bodily form into mine. This form was bright, almost piercingly white, and seemed to be made of pure, polished silver. This shape immediately merged with the inner gold of my body and disappeared under the skin of blossoms. At that moment I saw my angel standing behind me at the head of the coffin. What an entirely strange sensation! As if a blind spot was finally being revealed, shutters being taken down. Certainly not as if my angel had 'appeared' or entered the room, but much more as if I had finally, after decades of blindness, managed to look above my own head.

The physical state in which I found myself at this point is still a complete mystery to me. There was almost too much beauty and shining love within me to bear. Was it a vibration of pain or joy? Looking back I can only describe it as the purest form of a sun-body that I could conceive.

Yesterday I wrote that I was planning to do a talisman for my angel in Tiphareth, in order to reactivate my heart chakra and to support the process of transformation. The experience in the coffin tonight was so much more than that. It is a present from my angel to me, to us, and it will keep us in communion from now on. I have only to return in vision to the faceless body made of gold, with its skin of petals, and immediately I feel the closeness and the contact of my angel.

Brother Pollux, I will wax and wane, but you will remain. I will miss and fall, but you will stand; I will become blind and err, but you will see; I will waste and spend, but you will turn everything to gold. Even if some years from now I will not return to you more than a single gram, a grain of dust, then you will accept it and remain infinite in your love.

I guess, after all, that I did become the golem of my angel – and yet I still remain miles apart from it. Though a golem of clay is not the same as a golem of flowers. I am humbled and overjoyed. What begins from here is a path walked side by side. I will be able to overcome my perplexity only by beginning to share. Silence over the secret, but sharing the good fortune. What flowers can I sow? Where do I see ashes today? Where can I become an agent of such change? In every moment. I would have never thought it possible in this life. The tallest boundary between him and myself, between Castor on earth and Pollux in Hades, was the absence of my belief. It does not require a path; it requires acceptance.

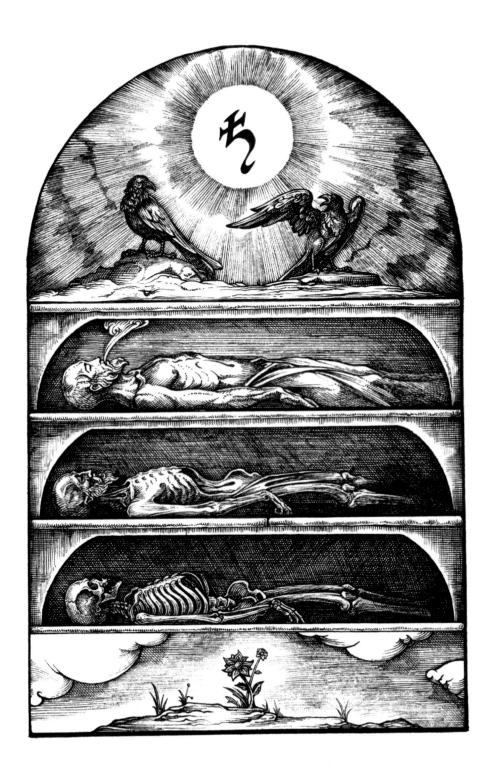

IV.IV.MMX

I am just returning from my first complete meditation, focused on strengthening my bond to Pollux and of the influx of the body of flowers. It did not require any groundwork or effort to return to conscious communion. Pollux again gave me the body of flowers; then he stood behind me and laid his hands (or something similar, as he doesn't have a corporeal body) on my shoulders. A current of deep peace and solar force filled me.

It was an incredible experience, so dense, weightless, and entirely without effort, as I held the contact. He is there whenever I let him be. It doesn't require any particular technique, any magic. Just silence and awareness of our communion.

VI.IV.MMX

Over the weekend I looked up the term Saturn gave me as advice for the time after the SatEx: HEVD. In volume 2 of *A Book of the Beginnings* by Gerald Massey, the word appears with the translation 'to be green, fresh, and hale.' An encouragement to see the world with fresh eyes and to further pursue many newfound perspectives.

Similarly impressively is that HEVD appears in Massey's book in the chapter on 'The Phenomenal Origin of Jehovah-Elohim'! IHVH Elohim, it seems, correlates directly with this advice, which makes particular sense as this divine name is the highest octave of Saturn. As this advice relates not only to all things Saturnine but also to the future of my life – or at least, that's how I like to interpret it – it makes sense that it was given by IHVH Elohim, and not Agiel for instance, who as the intelligence of Saturn is more one dimensional and rooted within Saturn alone.

What a wonderful farewell gift from the black brother, Saturn.

✳   ✳

✳

PART III

PRACTICE

SYSTASIS WITH YOUR HOLY DAIMON

It is necessary also that you should fully understand how you ought
to enjoy these immense riches, so that they may not be in your hands
unfruitful, or even harmful.

– The Book of Abramelin

Genuine Initiates do not grasp for powers they are unqualified to use
beneficially, but they do seek to extend their capacity for rightdoing, so
whatever power comes to them will be properly applied.

– William Gray, Inner Traditions of Magic

ANY PATHWAYS EXIST for achieving communion with your holy
daimon. Some of them are less costly than others, and most of
them have been forgotten today. What all of them have in common though, is that they require you to work on yourself first;
only then can you encounter another higher being. The focus of
the work moves from inward to outward. The raw stone has to
be finished before it can be set in its final position in the temple.
¶The journey towards communion with our holy daimon is a journey
towards fulfilment, towards becoming who we are meant to be and filling
with life every part of our patterned fate. This is the purpose to which our
personal daimon has been assigned to us, and if we want to connect to it
consciously then this is the journey to which we must dedicate ourselves.
The majority of this journey consists of the arduous task of transform-
ing our embodied personalities from obstacles to the work of our holy

daimon into partners and co-creators in that process. Despite the significance of such work, achieving it is the first step on an even longer journey.

> We do not have enough power at our own disposal to do anything very wonderful.[1]

What is really important to understand before we begin, is this: you are the interface through which communion with your holy daimon will ultimately be achieved. Your daimon is ready for communion, and has been since long before your birth. So it is not on her/him that you have to work, but on yourself. It is the interface between your daimon and the world that has to be refined. This interface is composed of your personality, or more specifically, the person you think you are at the moment. Once you have achieved communion, your work is to maintain this channel (i.e. your physical and spiritual senses) and keep it clear of anything that could impede it again.

I suggest four different stages to uncloak the voice and presence of your holy daimon. It would be wise to follow these stages in sequence, and work through each chapter in the order given. The work within each of these four stages is cyclical and will never end. Once we have finished the first cycle, we return to where we began, only in a slightly elevated position, and must then begin the next cycle of the operation. That's how we continually refine ourselves, and stay attuned to the level of consciousness where our holy daimon dwells. Despite this cyclical return, the expression of your practice will vary over time, and increasingly you'll discover your own methods. Slowly, without rushing, we transform ourselves from a vessel that receives to a vessel ready to give. The four stages are: Trust, Joy, Darkness and Encounter.

What I will present is the essential work, stripped bare of any romantic ideas, mysticism, or lodge affairs. Why? Because your daimon is a raw, pure, essential reality: it simply occupies a different realm. So let's mirror this in our work. Walking this path is not about our personal dreams, dramas, desires, or preferences. It is about the work that has to be done.

1 William Gray, *Inner Traditions of Magic*.

Nothing else. That work is to turn your senses into vehicles for, rather than obstacles to, the presence of your daimon.

Because this work will include a lot of teeth grinding and letting go of what you thought you were or needed, it is important to start this journey with an attitude of joyfulness. Though joy is the second stage of the initial cycle – let's do some teeth grinding first – it might be the most important stage of all. A joyful place is waiting for us; to get there the first step is to trust that we actually deserve to discover it. Let us begin with spiritualizing matter so we can become better agents of materializing spirit.

A Metaphor

OLLOWING THE HISTORICAL accounts given in previous chapters, and before we delve into actual practice, it is important to fill one last gap. That is, to equip us with a twenty-first century metaphor. This metaphor should feel a little more prosaic, a little closer to home. It should cut through the pages of the centuries and anchor us back in our own reality. So here is how I suggest you think of your relationship with your holy daimon:

Imagine a doctor who has a difficult disease to cure. The disease is hidden in the body of a patient. As the disease is widespread, the doctor cannot simply cut open the patient and take out the affected organs. The approach has to be more subtle, yet no less determined or effective. The doctor inserts a thin cable into the body of the patient. Attached to the end of the cable is a tiny device consisting of a camera and a laser. The recorded images from inside the patient's body are sent through the cable to a screen for the doctor to look at as he directs the device and operates on the patient.

Now this little setup in our imaginary operating theatre is all we need to get a more realistic picture of our relationship with our holy daimon. You, as in your current incarnated self, are the camera at the end of the tube. The doctor is your holy daimon. The patient is the world of creation into which you have been fully immersed. The beginning of this operation was the point of your first incarnation, and its end will be your last. Over the course of the entire operation the doctor will use many different cameras on the tube. However, both the screen and the hard drive that stores the camera's images will always be the same.

What can we take from this?

- First, there is no need for the holy daimon to 'talk' to the camera at the end of the tube. She/he is in control of it already. Even if they never see each other, their 'relationship' is perfectly fine. It 'just works.'
- Second, the only thing the doctor needs the camera to do is to 'record': to point the laser and follow the lead she/he is giving.
- Third, emotions don't play a role here. It doesn't matter if the camera finds what it records pleasant or unpleasant. Its only job is to explore the body of the patient objectively and operate on it successfully.
- Fourth, if the camera developed a conscious free will of its own and started to act independently from the doctor's lead, then it would mess up the operation. The camera has no idea where it is, why it was put there, or how deliberate actions to save something much bigger than it are being acted out through it.

What does this metaphor tell us about the process of gaining knowledge and conversation with our holy daimon? It tells us that there are a few operating principles we have to accept if we are to be successful:

First, gaining conscious contact with our holy daimon (the doctor) is not at all necessary for the successful completion of the operation. All organic life has the tendency to work just fine without human intervention. However, in fairness, under certain conditions having conscious access to one's holy daimon can be incredibly beneficial for the positive outcome of the operation.

To stay with our metaphor, that condition would be improving the quality of the interaction between doctor and camera by giving the camera a more conscious idea of the process in which it is involved. This means we need to be prepared to listen much more once we are connected to our holy daimon, and to talk less. The operating principles we can derive from this metaphor also demonstrate that the 'true will' of the camera is really the will of the doctor. The camera has to accept that it doesn't have the processing power to understand everything the doctor knows or intends to do. The camera can become a better version of itself, a more sophisticated tool; yet it can never become the doctor.

It should be noted that traditional approaches for achieving knowledge of our holy daimon (i.e. helping the camera see the doctor), such as the Saturn Rite given in this book and the much longer Abramelin ritual, are completely fine alternatives to the path we will lay out here. From the above it should be clear that the doctor doesn't really care how the camera becomes a better version of itself. She/he only cares about the clarity of the image that the camera can display, and how well its laser responds to her/his intent.

So while approaches such as my own or Abramelin work well, they can be significantly simplified. My journey took more than ten years, and it's only when looking back that I can see the many detours I took. The goal of this section is to simplify the approach, and get straight to business. Your holy daimon is talking to you already. All we need to do is to get you to a point where you are able to listen consciously to her/him and observe that she/he is working on you already.

✦

STAGE 1 · TRUST

Why Trust Matters

THE DESCRIPTION OF a landscape is called its topology. This word does not only describe physical landscapes; it can also describe the characteristics and details of a mental territory. When it is used in this way, any recurring feature, anything we consistently come across within a particular mental landscape (i.e. a specific time, culture, or region) is called a *topos*. Literary *topoi* (the plural of the Greek *topos*, 'place' or 'theme') are deeply embedded motifs that are foundational to the understanding of a particular culture or time.

When we look at our Western magical tradition (which is both oral and literary) as a landscape, we quickly realize that the concept of power is one of its most essential *topoi*.

From Prometheus to Faust, for more than twenty-five centuries magicians have been characterized by their disregard for social norms and rules in their pursuit of personal power. The nature of their lifelong voyages stood in stark contrast to the increasing levels of social regulation which slowly evolved into the threefold separation of powers (legislature, executive, judiciary) that all democratic governments respect today. Apotheosis or deification, the idea that an individual through their own choice, hard work, sweat and tears could raise themselves to a godlike stature, was the ultimate testament to the antisocial agenda of the magician.

In light of this it is no surprise that we find the magician standing at the crossroads of the paths of taboo and power. Countless generations of aspiring magicians have sought to leverage practices that are taboo, but which promise to increase their personal power. The chances were high that such an approach would get you quite far on your magical path – or at least on your way to the pyre. It is helpful to remind ourselves, that for centuries these two paths were one and the same.

Now, the kind of magic we are interested in here is of a very particular nature. Whether we call them *fravashis*, holy guardian angels, personal *daimones*, or something else, the object of our magic is the same: we want to establish a conscious communion between this being and ourselves. This significantly narrows down the magical techniques in which we are interested. We do not need to look at the vast majority of the West's magical literature, which concerns itself with such ends as healing warts, finding treasures, becoming invisible, stealing horses without getting caught, and bedding that special someone whose heart you have made yourself too small to believe you could ever win without magic.

The pursuit of magical power is both a necessity as well as a distraction. Over the centuries it has kept innumerable magicians from making any real progress in the Great Work. Gaining access to the poison of magical power, and learning to apply it with moderation and absolutely clear intent, is a skill that few of us will master in our lifetime. Without it we won't be able to achieve anything truly magical; yet once addicted to it this poison will equally keep us from creating anything meaningful beyond the narrow confines of our own ego. So at what point does this poison turn from a bare necessity into a dangerous distraction?

The answer is quite simple: Once you have acquired sufficient power to master yourself, you are ready to proceed into more complex areas of magic. For the kind of magic we are pursuing here, we are not trying to increase the power we have over the world at large; we are trying to increase the power we have over the world within ourselves. Ruling over our own elements, over the forces of life and destruction as they are sown into our blood, bones, and brain, and as they are woven into one beneath our skin – that is the whole premise of this stage of the Great Work.

What we gain from this process is the most foundational magical necessity of all: We stop being an obstacle in the Great Work and we become its most essential tool and source of power. We, as human beings, stop being part of the problem and finally become part of the solution. People who have mastered the art of handling magical power without getting addicted to its poison have developed a set of core skills that I would describe like this. They have a proven and genuine trust in the following abilities:

· To get shit done if they set their will to it.
· To not get carried away in the process of doing so.
· To stay focused over long periods of time.
· To be okay with failing often and coming back to try again.

What we are talking about here is no magic at all, yet without these skills, no magic will ever come from you. And dangerously, seeing this process work in the world can become a drug in itself. Have you ever watched young boys play in the woods? Having been one of them long ago, I can tell you that they love breaking branches, carving bark, chopping down saplings, and generally destroying anything their small bodies allow them to. Obviously this is not because they are bad kids, but because this is their playful way of experiencing self-efficacy – the ability to apply oneself to the world and leave a mark. If this kind of immediate feedback and gratification loop is still required as an adult, then we are caught in the vicious circle of reproducing the same behaviour over and over again, still caught in the childish hope that breaking this or breaking that will ultimately create a higher degree of trust in ourselves. But it doesn't. And being hooked on seeing how we leave a dent in the world will make for a pretty dented world. We have to learn how to put our power into the service of something greater than ourselves.

To become a magician we have to become a gateway for significant (spiritual, elemental, celestial, chthonic, you name it) power. Handling these forces is actually quite straightforward, so long as we do not desire to abuse them to prove our human self-efficacy to the world. The level of magical power you'll be able to handle successfully depends more than anything on your ability to remove yourself from the equation. This is neither an act of servile self-denial nor of divine bondage: it is about trusting that you'll be okay whatever happens.

*

Exercises in Trust

S O LET'S FOCUS on a few ways to develop trust in our ability to handle magical powers without getting stuck in the game. At the heart of these exercises lies the skill of quickly switching one's mode of presence, or better, being present in two modes at once. Here we will focus on the opposing modes of 'holding onto' and 'letting go of.' ¶ First we need to become comfortable with handling a significant amount of power. Once we have become comfortable with this, we need to switch mode and become equally comfortable with letting go of that power. We need to trust in our ability to shift between and be successfully present in both states, powerless and powerful.

Practising this skill in magic is hard, which is why we'll aim to introduce it as playfully as possible. And yet, once you have understood this concept, you'll have laid a foundation for your future practice that too few magicians accomplish these days. This foundation will serve you well in both magical and mundane life. In leadership training this skill is called 'polarity management,' and in Gestalt coaching it is called 'finding the middle mode.'

STRETCHING YOUR POLARITIES

You can do this exercise anywhere: in public or in private, alone or in a crowd. It can be done in less than a minute, and should be practised little and often. Do not underestimate its impact just because it seems so plain and inconspicuous.

Open your left hand and let it rest gently wherever it is placed. Bring your consciousness into it and slowly allow all tension to fade from its muscles. Just as you would put a child to bed at night, carefully lay your left hand to rest. Or if you are walking, let it move gently with the motion of your body. Give it space, and allow it to be present and entirely unconstrained. You might want to reflect on the nature of your open hand. Maybe you'll think something like this: 'This is a hand. It is an open hand. In being entirely itself it also is the gestalt of all hands that have ever been. This is a hand. It happens to be attached to my body. Through it flows the history of everything all hands have ever done on this planet. This is the open hand.' Let your left hand rest calmly in this state, and bring your focus to your right hand.

Form the fingers of your right hand together into a fist. Slowly, while keeping your left hand relaxed, increase the muscular tension in your right hand. Let your fist become tighter and tighter. Let your fingertips press hard into the flesh of your palm. Feel how the power of your body is increasingly being drawn and absorbed by your right hand. Keep building and holding this strength in your right hand. If you are walking, your right hand should no longer be moving with your body, but be firm as a rock at your side. Now keep on walking like this, or sitting wherever you are.

You might want to reflect on the nature of your fist. Maybe you'll think something like this: 'This is a fist. It is a building tool. It is a killing tool. The force that forms this fist is the force of all of creation. Rocks and metals and oceans are all formed by this force, held together now by my bones, muscles, and flesh. This is a fist. It is attached to my body. Yet through it flows the history of everything that has ever been done with a fist. This is the fist.'

Then, keeping your left hand relaxed and your right fist under tension, stop concentrating on them. You are neither your left hand nor your right hand. You are in between them. You are the bridge that links them together. Stay in this space for as long as you want. Feel the presence of your hands in their opposite states. Feel yourself, breathing, holding on and letting go, right inbetween them.

Then let go of both states. Notice how quickly both hands return to a state of comfort and normality. Now they are neither fully relaxed nor fully strained. Your hands are wise. They are already experts in handling the poison of power. They know so perfectly well how to mix tension and calmness that you hardly ever notice them doing it.

TWO MODES OF TRATAK

This exercise takes a little longer, and you will need a dark, windless and undisturbed place for it. Just as with the previous exercise, it's best to work on this skill little and often. Ideally you can practice Mode 1 in the morning and Mode 2 in the evening. You can also do both exercises at the same time each day for no less than five minutes each.

Mode 1

Sit in a dark place and light a candle. Place it in front of you so that you can easily see its flame while your eyes are relaxed. Now gaze at the flame without moving. Do not move your hands, swallow or blink. Just sit and gaze motionlessly at the flame. When you are ready, close your eyes and focus on the flame's negative imprint on your retina. Inside or outside, it does not matter; the flame is still with you and you are with it. When your vision of the flame fades, open your eyes again and refresh it, not moving anything except your eyelids.

See how long you can practice in this manner. Five minutes is good; several hours (just for the stage with open eyes) is getting closer to expert level. Also, do not worry if your eyes begin to water as you stare without blinking. This is a natural and healthy way for the eye to clean itself and keep your retina covered with the film of fluid that is renewed by blinking.

Keep a record in your magical diary of your observations about this exercise. Helpful questions for exploration could be: What is a flame? How much of yourself can you merge with the flame? When you are one with the flame, how do you perceive the space surrounding the flame? Where does the flame go when the candle is extinguished?

Mode 2

For this exercise you will need two candles. Light both of them and place them to your far left and right respectively. Position them in such way that you can just about hold both flames in the corners of your field of vision. You do not need to see them clearly: they should be on the edge of your peripheral vision. Rest your gaze in the centre and perceive both flames at once. Aim to hold both flames in your visual field without seeing either of them clearly. When you are ready, you can close your eyes and continue the exercise on the inside. Behind your eyelids, gaze at the peripheral impression the flames have left on your retina. When your vision of the flames fades, open your eyes again and refresh it.

As with the previous exercise, make notes in your magical diary and continue to add observations as you progress with your practice. Helpful questions for exploration could be: What is the space that exists between the two flames? What do you merge with by not focusing on either of them? How does this exercise affect you differently from the previous one? What is similar?

Mode 1 strengthens your focused vision, Mode 2 teaches you peripheral or open vision. The latter mode of viewing tends to be much harder to get accustomed to. Mode 2 has also been called 'eternity gaze.'

Should you want to learn more about these gaze-meditation techniques then start by researching the Sanskrit term *tratak*. Unlike the purpose of traditional *tratak*-methods, the intent here is not primarily to become expert at either mode of vision, but to experience the difference between them, to become acquainted with them, and most importantly to develop the ability to easily switch between them. Just as we are neither the open hand nor the closed fist, so we are neither the focused vision nor the peripheral one.

THE SERPENT AND THE EGG

Phanes, the Orphic primeval deity of new life hatched from an egg with a serpent wound about it, has been called the 'Revealer'; and indeed new wisdom awaits us by learning more about this mystical image. The serpent wound about the egg has been an object of gnostic reflection for many centuries. Countless times it has been hammered into stone, painted in oil, tattooed on skin, or conjured in vision.

Before we begin this third exercise in Trust, let's take a moment to meditate on the body of the serpent. Can you see the polarity here? The painful and deeply personal dilemma of the snake? At every moment the serpent has to make a decision. Should it continue to incubate the egg with the warmth of its coiled body, or should it tighten its muscles just a little more and break its fragile shell? The snake's immediate desire is to break it: serpents love devouring fresh eggs. Yet it can choose to resist this desire, even though this means resisting its every instinct. Instead of breaking the egg, it can choose to turn its body into a tool of generation and creation. But this is a process with high stakes. It would leave the snake hungry for a long time, and there is no guarantee of success. After all, no snake has ever before witnessed an egg hatch. So this is the snake's choice: how should it apply the power that was granted to it? To

foster destruction or creation? To feed itself or feed new life? To follow its desire, or to resist it and follow a path into uncertainty?

For this exercise you will need two eggs. Either both should be raw, or one should be hard-boiled; I would recommend that you start with one raw and one hard-boiled egg.

This exercise should be done in the morning, before your day begins. Sit in a quiet place. Place the two eggs before you, just as you placed the single candle in the previous exercises. You should be able to see them clearly while keeping your eyes relaxed. When your mind and body have settled into calm and silence, pick up the raw egg. Hold it in your hands and meditate on it. Here are a few guiding questions to explore: What is the nature of an egg? Where did the perfect smoothness of its shell come from? Is the world captured inside the egg, or is the world surrounding the egg? And what about your hands holding it? Are you now the serpent, ready either to incubate the seed of life or to break its shell? How many eggs have you broken unthinkingly in your life before? Who are you to the egg?

When your mind has fully explored the egg, its nature, and your relationship with it, take a deep breath. Then, without hesitation, throw the egg forcefully on the floor before you.

Settle back into your position of calm, look at the broken egg, and continue your meditation. What are your thoughts now? Maybe you want to reflect on these questions: Where did the power to break this egg come from? Where does it rest in your body when it is not being used? When in your life have you used this sort of destructive power before? What do you see now about the dangers of being you?

When your exploration has ended, clean up the broken egg and get ready for your day. When you are about to start, return to your meditation place and pick up the second egg. Now you'll reverse your earlier decision, and rather than breaking the second egg you will carry it with you, in your left or right hand, for an entire day. Your goal is to incubate it with the warmth of your palms to learn about the sacrifice it takes to gestate and protect new life.

You'll realize that protecting life is much harder than destroying it. In my own practice, I gave myself permission to place the egg next to my hands when holding it was impossible, for instance when I was driving or writing. Now you will realize why I recommended that you boil the second egg at first! You might find yourself riding a bike with an egg in your hand, sitting in meetings with an egg in your hand, having lunch or dinner with an egg in your hand – and of course people asking you why you have an egg in your hand. My default answer was always this: 'I am doing a mindfulness course, and this is part of my training. I need to be mindful of this egg over the course of an entire day and bring it home safely again.'

✳

Reflections on Trust

I N THESE EXERCISES we have exposed ourselves to three polarities: the polarity of power in our bodies, the polarity of mastering that power without becoming attached to it, and the polarity of creation and destruction that sits at the heart of so many of our decisions, whether mundane or magical. ¶ When you have done these exercises, you may find yourself faced with the single most important question that can emerge from them. It should be obvious by now that this question is not: 'Do I have sufficient power at my disposal, and if not, how can I increase it?' Rather, it is the more intimate question: 'Can I trust myself? Whatever power is accessible to me right now, can I trust myself to handle it wisely? What reason do I have to believe that I am fully qualified to balance my desire with my will?' There are three reasons why your personal answer to this question matters so much:

1 Achieving communion with your holy daimon will significantly change how you'll have to work with power as a magician. It will also significantly increase the force and volume of power that will flow into you as a vessel. Are you properly prepared to handle these forces? Or will they break you? The answer to this has nothing to do with stamina or strength, but with the firmness of your ethics and the flexibility with which you apply yourself to an ever-changing world.

2 Achieving communion with your holy daimon is no mean feat. It is a feat that few magicians in any generation achieve. One of the main blocks for those who don't achieve it is that deep under their skin, in the quiet of their own heart, they inherently doubt that they could ever really do it. They haven't developed enough trust in their ability to get shit done in this world before attempting to achieve something that is out of this world. If you don't want to number yourself among them, then learn to handle polarities really well, rather than trying to increase the amount of power available to you. First apply what you have learned to this world, before stepping forward into the magical realm.

3 Finally, achieving communion with your holy daimon is a feat which no-one else will ever be able to assess. Even after years of successful work in conscious conjunction with your holy daimon, your physical eye will still never have seen it; nor will your physical hands ever have touched it. Trust plays a crucial role here: do you trust yourself enough to stay honest with yourself throughout this journey? Are you gentle enough with yourself when you fail, and strict enough when you risk getting carried away? Do you trust yourself to judge yourself without emotion, and in the absence of any other kind of orientation?

The answer to all three of these questions literally rests in the palm of your hand as you carry an unbroken egg through a busy day of work or study. It is also reassuring to know that all our ancestors struggled with this same essential question. The seventeenth century mystic Jakob Böhme provided me with some of my deepest meditations on what it truly means to generate the necessary readiness within oneself to successfully channel the force he called 'magia.' The following quote is taken from his *Six Points On Mysticism* (*Sex Puncta Mystica*). Here he defines the most essential components of magic, or magia:

> Magia is the mother of eternity, the being of all beings, because she creates herself and is understood in Desire. Within herself she is nothing but a Will; the same Will is the Great Mystery of all wonders and secrecy. (...) The Desire, however, creates such a nature in the Will so that the Will is within itself. The true magia is not a being, but the desiring spirit of the being. She is a matrix without substance and yet reveals itself in being.[2]

Böhme's language is hard to decipher, but if we read it slowly and carefully enough, then its meaning reveals itself. Böhme explains that magic is not a force embedded in nature, but rather it is the heart of nature itself. It is a force that has no substance in itself, but it allows all substance to come into existence. It is the cosmic, patterning power that leads to all

---

2 Jakob Böhme, 407, translated by Frater Acher.

being and creation. This is why Böhme called magic 'the mother of eternity,' for all created beings, in their eternal waves of coming and going, are her offspring.

Following this introduction, Böhme offers an unambiguous clue as to how we humans can connect with this process of constant weaving and patterning and become its co-creators: it is by mastering the twin forces of desire and will. The former is the fire within which we forge the latter. Then, one day, the latter becomes the hand that holds tightly to the former. According to Böhme, getting ready to handle magia successfully is a side-effect of mastering one's desire and will and combining them in one balanced vessel of power.

Obviously the work of acquiring this skill is not limited to our magical practice. All aspects of our life, even the most mundane, must become laboratories for our work. While getting ready to handle significant amounts of magical power may be our goal, the bulk of the work to achieve this must be conducted on the periphery of our magical lives.

The English word 'power' has its root in the Latin *posse*, 'to be able to.' With any new skill, the power we ultimately gain from mastering it is not what we focus on while we are in the process of acquiring it. What we must focus on when we learn a new skill are the countless small movements that comprise it, movements that we need to replicate, sequence, and combine. As Böhme tells us, the core skills of magic are to be gained by mastering our desire and will: tools that when placed in the hands of man will propogate or destroy the seeds of life.

> Mystery is nothing other than the magical will, which still lies caught in desire. (...) The Magician has power in this Mystery to act according to his will, and can do what he pleases. But he must be armed in that element wherein he would create; else he will be cast out as a stranger, and given into the power of the spirits thereof, to deal with him according to their desire.[3]

3 Jakob Böhme.

137

STAGE 2 · JOY

Why Joy Matters

ACHIEVING COMMUNION with your holy daimon is supposed to be hard magical work. The story of the *Book of Abramelin* begins with the Jew Abraham of Worms going on a quest that takes him far out of his comfort zone, away from all familiar lands and out into the Egyptian desert. What does joy matter on this journey? Well, it matters a lot. And in this chapter we will explore why, and how, we can equip ourselves with this powerful shield.

> I both have exhorted, and do exhort unto a solitary life, which is the source of all good; it is true that it is difficult to accustom oneself thereunto; but once thou shalt have obtained the Sacred Science and Magic the love for retirement will come unto thee of thine own accord, and thou wilt voluntarily shun the commerce with and conversation of men; for the pleasure and contentment thou wilt enjoy when thou shalt be the possessor of this Science will be so great that thou wilt despise all amusements, excursions, riches, and every other thing however attractive such may be.[4]

Achieving communion with your holy daimon will require periods of isolation and withdrawal. And as Abraham of Worms, the alleged author of the *Book of Abramelin* said, isolation 'is difficult to accustom oneself' to. He also said that it was easy once you have 'obtained the Sacred Science and Magic.' But how do we accustom ourselves to the difficulties of this path before we have acquired the divine tools magic has to offer? This is where joy comes in.

Think of yourself as a vessel. Normally this vessel is being continuously filled with water from many sources, and thus is in a state of overflowing sensual experience. New water pours in while old water flows out, and there is a neverending coming and going of experiences, some delightful

---

4 *The Book of Abramelin.*

and others painful, some of them indifferent and many invisible to our conscious minds.

When we go into isolation, we stop all of this. We deliberately create emptiness and openness within us. We make of ourselves an untouched space, an empty vessel that attracts the attention of all sorts of spiritual beings who would love to take up residence in it and fill it with their own waters. It offers shelter and food and richness to all the spiritual beings who cannot provide these things for themselves, who prey on carrion. And carrion is exactly what such energy is to them.

So in isolation we strive to empty our vessel of new impressions. We strive to empty it of our senses, both mental and physical. We create an empty space that will ultimately be used by our holy daimon to create a conscious communion with us. However, until then we must guard this empty vessel and ensure that we don't get tricked and abused by other beings who would prey on our openness. This is why we seal this vacant space with joy.

The type of joy we mean is the most wonderful protective seal. Joy is the shield that shines like the sun. And just like the sun it has no source but is self-sustaining: we have but to learn to ignite it within ourselves.

Once we have experienced real joy, we'll see how vastly different it is from the other contemplative emotions experienced in seclusion such as melancholia, nostalgia, and daydreaming. None of these can work as a protective seal on our empty vessel. Quite the opposite, in fact. Melancholia, nostalgia and daydreaming are red carpets rolled out for beings who would take up residence in the vessel of our mind. For as long as we are attached to these emotional states, our vessel cannot be considered empty.

Finally, a word of caution. It is true that when we encounter our holy daimon an incredible source of joy and wellbeing is unlocked for us. However, in many cases this source doesn't open like a floodgate; more often what comes through is a little trickle that only moistens the ground. Later we might notice its waters between the rocks and plants, and much later it becomes a slowly broadening stream. That is, assuming we have kept up our practice and remained in touch with our holy daimon. Eventually, that small creek will have grown deep and broad enough for us to be carried upon it out into the ocean.

Exercises in Joy

It seemed to me as though I was listening to a Voice, not human but celestial, and I felt a joy in mine heart such as I could not express.

– The Book of Abramelin

(...) for it is absolutely necessary to perform this Operation unto the praise, honour, and glory of God.

– The Book of Abramelin

I N RECENT DECADES significant efforts have been made in our Western societies to regain access to the kind of joy which we are dealing with here, the joy that seals the empty space of our minds. Most of the techniques and pathways that were revived as part of this trend stem from the Far East, and today they are easily accessible through articles, books, workshops, and mobile apps. We find them filed under topics such as meditation, mindfulness, and, more broadly, wellbeing.

The chances are that you will already have some personal experience of these approaches. If not, let me encourage you to explore these powerful techniques for yourself. Building up proper meditation skills and keeping our body and mind attuned to them is a journey that is never finished, but rather is a process of constant refinement. We should not, therefore, be reticent to start out on such a journey at any point in our lives, whether we are fifteen or fifty, and whether our lives are currently calm or caught in a swirling storm. However, here we wish to explore something quite different. From the stream of our collective past we want to help recover an ancient practice that has not yet received the same level of attention as its quiet sibling, meditation. While it is closely related to other mindfulness exercises, this ancient technique in some respects runs quite contrary to them. It is deeply rooted in our Western magical tradition, and thus of particular interest to our current study. It is part of a body of practice that it would greatly benefit Western magicians to remember and reawaken. And the way into this practice can be found in a most unexpected place.

Our human hubbub, which invites everything in, all of the light, the music, all madness of thought and all shades of pain, the wealth of memory and the wealth of expectations, it is only shut to one thing: to unity. In every glance a thousand further lurking glances blink who do not want to become closely united; every fair and pure amazement is confused by a thousand memories; and even in the innermost silent sorrow a thousand questions whisper. The hubbub is lush and scant, it amounts to abundance and refuses embrace, it builds a whirl of objects and a whirl of emotions, whirlwind to whirlwind, making it fly over and against each other, and it makes us pass through, all while on this our own path, devoid of unity.[5]

Only there is a kind of experience which arises from the soul itself, without touch and without obstruction, in its naked own being. It becomes and accomplishes itself beyond the everyday hubbub, free of the other, inaccessible to the other. It does not require sustenance and no poison can reach it. The soul, who stands within it, stands within itself, belongs to itself, experiences itself boundlessly. Not any longer because it is has subjected itself entirely to an object of the world, not because it has summoned itself within an object of the world it experiences itself as the unity, but because it has immersed itself entirely in itself, it has dived down deep on its own bed, pit and husk, sun and eye, drunkard and drink in one. This innermost experience is what the Greek called *ekstasis*, the stepping outside.[6]

The term 'ecstasy' is a combination of the words *ek*, 'out' and *histanai*, 'to place, cause to stand.' So in its original form the term defined a state in which one had left one's proper place, one had shifted outside of one's normal perspective. In the seventeenth century European mystical writers began to use the word to describe a state of rapture that numbed the body while the soul was in gnosis and experienced the divine. Over time the

---

5 Martin Buber, *Ekstatische Konfessionen*, §.11.
6 Martin Buber, *Ekstatische Konfessionen*, §.12.

meaning of the word shifted to a more general positive notion of an exalt-
ed state of good feeling.

Just like entering inner calm, entering ecstasy is an art form. But unlike
the inner calm now taught in meditation and mindfulness classes around
the globe, no modern trend has yet revived the ancient techniques of
mystical ecstasy in the West. This is why ecstasy is largely misunderstood
as the opposite of calmness. And that is also why the kind of ecstasy we
are dealing with here has been almost entirely forgotten.

One of the last active Western communities to know about the power
of this kind of spiritual state, as well as the particular practices to induce and use it practically, were the eighteenth century Polish Hasidim,
founded by the enigmatic Rabbi Yisroel ben Eliezer (c.1700–1760), often
called the Baal Shem Tov. Just as their name refers to the fourth sephirah,
Chesed, so their entire communal lifestyle, which promoted kindness and
piety, aimed to bring principles of (Lurianic) Kabbalah into the experience of daily life.

The great German Jewish philosopher Martin Buber, at the beginning
of the twentieth century, began to collect and publish their mystical tales
which contained the living memories of these communities and their holy
tzadikim, or 'righteous ones.' For practitioners of Western magic the importance of these half-fictional records cannot be overestimated. For centuries the magical tradition of the West was an underground movement
practised at the periphery of European society. Whenever it dared to
surface or to come too close to the centre of society, it was persecuted and
its records and practitioners burned. Many of its artefacts were encrypted
or reduced to the bare bones of ritual instructions and recipes. As a result
of this process, the literary tradition of Western magic lost much of its
poetry and much of its practical connection to individual and communal
reality. Such is the fissure which the accounts of the mystical Hasidic tales
can somewhat begin to heal for us.

While the early Hasidim themselves were not practising magicians,
many of their holy men were experienced mystics. The way they incorpo-
rated deeply magical and mystical principles into their everyday lives is entirely unique and deeply educational for any modern Western practitioner.
This is also why many critics have held that Hasidism is 'less of a world-

view than a religious technique. The main tool of its magic is the prayer.[7]

The Polish Hasidim had not only a wonderful word for the kind of ecstasy we are exploring here, but also a deeply entrenched practice to access it. They called it *hitlahavut*. Derived from the Hebrew *l-h-v, lahav*, 'burning, flame, to be inflamed,' the word illustrates the primal principle of Hasidic life in the idea of a burning within the practitioner.[8] Buber, in his introduction to *The Legend of the Baal-Shem*, explains that this inner light must be lit through a combination of divine love, fear, and fervour. The *Oxford Dictionary of the Jewish Religion* describes the power of such a spiritual state: 'profound joy in God is rooted in an inner fervour – *hitlahavut* – from which one can achieve complete self-effacement.'[9]

Now we can understand why *hitlahavut* has not yet made it into the Western mainstream. Unlike mindfulness, and most Westernised forms of meditation, it cannot be stripped from its deeply spiritual foundation. *Hitlahavut* has a truly unruly nature, mystical fervour cannot be accessed before one has had a highly intimate and initiatory spiritual experience; and neither does it accept the confines of religious orthopraxy or orthodoxy. This kind of joy, therefore, is both a deeply mystical principle and one that by definition promotes 'religious anarchism.'[10] In the introduction to his *Ecstatic Confessions*, Martin Buber gives us this beautiful first-person account of *hitlahavut*:

> I am the dark side of the moon: you know about my existence, yet what you determine for the bright side does not apply to me. I am the remainder of the equation, that which does not come out even. You may impose a sign on me, but you cannot resolve me.[11]

But how, then, do we light this flame within us? Or in other words, how do we walk out onto the dark side of the moon? The key to this for the Hasidim was found in their particular practice of prayer. However, the

---

7 Friedrich Gundolf, in Bourel, 157.
8 Urban, 125.
9 Berlin, 352.
10 Urban, 125.
11 Martin Buber, *Ekstatische Konfessionen*, 5.

kind of prayer that they regarded so highly was quite distinct from earlier Jewish mystical traditions. Unlike the intricate letter combinations of an Abraham Abulafia, the Hasidim promoted an entirely non-intellectual way of approaching the divine through ecstasy. In a famous story the Baal Shem Tov praised the unlearned young son of a shepherd who at the height of the Yom Kippur prayers in the synagogue could no longer hold back his fervour, and, as he could not yet read the prayers, took out his flute and played it in the synagogue. The Baal Shem, in his wisdom, rather than condemning the boy for interrupting that most holy moment of their prayers, praised him before the whole community. It was the pure, burning melody of the shepherd son's flute, he said, that had finally raised everyone else's prayer into the heavens. The story concludes that 'every service which proceeds from a simple or a unified soul is sufficient and complete.'[12]

This kind of ecstasy is not bound to erudition, ritual, or religious tradition. Instead, for the soul to catch fire and become a sun, we have to discover ways to empower our hearts to speak directly to the divine world, as well as to be spoken to.

✳

12 Buber, *The Legend of the Baal-Shem*, 18.

Igniting Your Hitlahavut

One who rejoices, utters not words, but it is a certain sound of joy with-
out words: for it is the expression of a mind poured forth in joy, express-
ing, as far as it is able, the affection, but not compassing the feeling.
— St Augustine on spiritual singing, Exposition on Psalm 100

THE HUMAN VOICE is one of the most powerful magical tools. It can resound in the world around us or silently within us; and it is the one tool that has always been considered essential for prayer. It is also the most efficient tool for igniting the dormant force of *hitlahavut* within us. To practice this, you'll need a remote place where your singing cannot be overheard. If you do not have the luxury of a suitable indoor space then find an outdoor place that does. You would not be the first magician who has spent hours in the woods at night practising this core skill.

One of the biggest stumbling blocks for learning to sing magically is the thought of how you sound to other people. But you are not singing for others; you are singing to make your body vibrate at the particular frequency that elevates mind, body, flesh, and blood.

The most essential quality of this sort of singing is that it heals. It heals ourselves, and it heals the beings around us. The very vibrations of our voice can mend the broken, open the closed, and erect the fallen. But the intention behind those vibrations is also important, as is the fire of fervour that it ignites in us and in the world around us. The kind of singing we are pursuing speaks to the flesh, the spirits, and the gods. The only reason we don't call it praying is to avoid the associations of that word. For many of us, the word 'prayer' smells of hierarchy, tradition, structure, and a path that thousands have already trodden over the centuries. Magical singing is not like this. It is entirely ephemeral and unique to you. Some sounds you will produce once in your life and then never again. Some melodies will be given to you to unlock a specific moment, gate, or being, and you'll forget them before the echo of your voice has faded. Magical singing lives; each of us must find our own version of it.

Much has been written about the magical use of the psalms, and there is a long tradition in the West of linking certain psalms to specific magical acts and artefacts. There are books dedicated to the subject, such as the *Sepher Shimmush Tehillim*, and many grimoires employ psalms as protective charms, often inscribed on seals and around magical circles.

You will use individual lines from psalms to train the flow and vibration of your voice. Do not consider this a traditional Christian or Jewish practice; it is not, it is your own. Direct your song only at your heart, your hands, and your blood. It can echo out into the world on its own.

Choose a line from a psalm that particularly resonates with you. This can be done by taking a Bible, opening it randomly in Psalms, and seeing what line immediately jumps out. Don't overthink this. Letting yourself follow little coincidences as they arise is a good attitude when you are easing yourself into this practice.

Commit the line to memory, then go to your remote space where your singing cannot be overheard or disturbed. You may prefer to sit somewhere quietly or go for a walk: it does not matter at this point. Later, though, it would be beneficial to stand or sit calmly in your mediation position, with an upright back, a relaxed chest, a lengthened neck and spine, and wearing nothing that could constrain your breathing or vocal chords. When the time is right, begin to sing your line. Don't try to create anything beautiful or particularly meaningful, just let your voice play with the words.

Singing a statement of magical intent can grow to become one of the most powerful and immediate forms of magic open to us. Spirits love (or depending on the song and their nature, fear) listening to the voice of humans. The human voice, if used well, is capable of creating all-vibrating rays of power that can stir, sublimate or separate spirit and substance. And most importantly, the physical human voice is something entirely out of the reach of spirits. The spoken word is the sword blade of the magician. It forms the bridge between the realm of the spirits and the realm of matter. It is itself a hybrid power, half born of flesh, half born of spirit. Singing – making our voice carry particular melodies and vibrations that express intent not only in the words spoken but also in the meaning of the melody – is a force not many beings or objects in creation can resist.

You'll easily be able to track your progress in your training. Here are just a few ways of measuring some of the milestones on this particular path of practice:

1 When you sing, in which parts of your body do you feel your voice most clearly? As you tune and alter your voice, can you feel how different parts of your body start to resonate? Can you map the resonance of the five vowels to particular parts of your body?

2 When you sit in silence after practising singing, what do you sense? How long does the echo of your voice remain with you? What other thoughts come to you? How is this experience altered by different lines from Psalms?

3 How well can you maintain the impact of your voice when you sing softly? How quietly can you sing while keeping your voice impacting fully on yourself and the world around you?

4 When you sing can you use your voice as a tool on the world around you? With your eyes closed, can you direct it to touch or interact with objects in your imagination and in the space around you? How do you see your voice in vision? Is it a light, a pattern, or a mixture of both?

I am about to say what ye know. One who jubilates, utters not words, but it is a certain sound of joy without words: for it is the expression of a mind poured forth in joy, expressing, as far as it is able, the affection, but not compassing the feeling. A man rejoicing in his own exultation, after certain words which cannot be uttered or understood, bursts forth into sounds of exultation without words, so that it seems that he indeed does rejoice with his voice itself, but as if filled with excessive joy cannot express in words the subject of that joy... Those who are engaged at work in the fields are most given to jubilate; reapers, or vintners, or those who gather any of the fruits of the earth, delighted with the abundant produce, and rejoicing in the very richness and exuberance of the soil, sing in exultation; and among the songs which they utter in words, they put in certain cries without words in the exultation of a rejoicing mind; and this is what is meant by jubilating.[13]

13 St Augustine, *Expositions on the Psalms.*

Singing with the Planets

Spells can draw the moon down from the skies.

– Virgil[14]

Song is the most potent imitator of all. (...) When song, with equal power, imitates heavenly things, the stimulus is amazing – for our spirit to accept heaven's influence and for the influence to reach our spirit. But the very material of singing is purer and much more like the heavens than medicinal: this material is air (...). Singing, therefore, full of spirit and sense – if the song responds to this star or to that one by its meanings, by its linkages and the form resulting from them, and also by the effect of the imagination – transfers from sources to the singer, and from him to the listener nearby, no less power than anything else that can be put together, as long as the singing sustains its strength and the singer's spirit.

– Marsilio Ficino[15]

W HAT WE ARE TRYING to accomplish here is something quite simple: singing while bathing in the light of a particular planet. We will see what happens, take notes, choose a different planet, and compare our results. It is like learning the stages of a musical scale, where our voice is the string, our (spiritual and physical) bodies the sound box, and the planets the conductors.

First, decide on the planet in whose presence you'll be singing. We recommend focusing your practice in particular on the Sun, as this is the planet with which we will continue to work in the following exercise. Determine the position of this planet relative to your position at the time that you will practise. Today this can be easily done with mobile apps. For this exercise we do not recommend that you use psalms to guide your singing. At this point you should allow your voice to be guided by the experience itself. Whether you sing actual words, long sequences of vowels,

---

14 Virgil (70–19 BCE), Eclogue 8.64, quoted in Copenhaver, 124.
15 Marsilio Ficino (1433–1499), *Three Books on Life*, 3.21, in Copenhaver, 364–365.

self-made 'barbaric' words, or switch between all three is of no concern. Rather than trying to find the 'right' psalm that matches the planet of your choice, meditate again on the quote of Martin Buber on ecstasy as the 'dark side of the moon' or the one from St Augustine on jubilation as 'a certain sound of joy without words.'

Should you still want to begin your practice with the use of a psalm, you should choose one that corresponds to the spirit of the planet with which you'll be working. Suitable psalms are inscribed around some of the planetary pentacles in the *Key of Solomon*. But here is a warning: should you indeed want to experiment with these psalms, you must not use the psalms related to Jupiter and Saturn for this exercise. Even Venus or Mars are better left for later. For your initial stage of learning, concentrate your time and experience on the psalms corresponding to Moon and Sun.

Moon: Psalm 56:11
In God I trust; I will not be afraid. What can mere humans do to me?

Venus: Psalm 22:14
I am poured out like water, and all my bones are disjointed; my heart is like wax, melting within me.

Mercury: Psalm 24:7
Lift up your heads, you gates! Rise up, ancient doors! Then the King of glory will come in.

Sun: Psalm 91:11–12
For he will order his angels to care for you and guard you wherever you go. They will carry you in their hands, so that you won't trip on a stone.

Mars: Psalm 110:5
The Lord is at your right hand; he will crush kings on the day of his anger.

Jupiter: Psalm 112:3
Wealth and riches are in his house, and his righteousness endures forever.

Saturn: Psalm 18:7
Then the earth shook and quaked; the foundations of the mountains trembled, they shook because he burned with anger.

Go to your remote space where you cannot be disturbed or overheard, and find somewhere to sit comfortably. Ground yourself in silence and presence using the meditation technique of your choice, one of the tratak exercises described above, or the Meditation of the Void.[16]

With your eyes closed, visualise the location of the planet you are working with relative to your body. Then reach out to this planet and draw it down into your presence. The term 'drawing down' is often used in magic, particularly in Wiccan circles. What this means is to establish a sound and undisturbed connection between yourself and the target of your attention. Your exact process for drawing down a planet will depend on your skills and experience. Simply reach out for the planet in its current position and pull it towards you. On occasion you may find yourself close to an ancient celestial object in all its massiveness and radiance. Whatever happens, trust your vision to guide you.

When the time is right and you are within the planet's light, begin to sing to it. As your voice finds it path, gently guide it towards, or even into, the body of the planet. Once you have both tuned into each other, witness what is happening around you. How do your voice and the light of the planet interact? What happens to your body, both in vision and physically? If nothing happens at first, don't worry; simply continue to sing. And remember not to hold on to the structure or melody of your voice. You are just the string and the sound box, the planet is the conductor.

A word of caution. The longest I ever managed to sing for a planet was close to an hour. It left me completely exhausted and vulnerable to this planet's influence for many years to come. Do not impose any artificial goals on yourself as part of this practice, such as singing for all seven planets at least once or for a certain amount of time. Remember, it is not about how much power is available to us, but the agility and flexibility with which we can respond to such power. In magic, most of the really

16 A recording is available at www.josephinemccarthy.com/audio-file-archive.

important work happens at the periphery, which in this case is once the singing has stopped.

Before moving on, be sure to note down your observations carefully in your magical diary. You might find it helpful to reflect on the following questions: How did the planet respond to your singing? How did its response affect your body as well as your voice? Did you see the planet's light in your vision? And more specifically, did you witness any kind of patterns or currents in the space between you and the planet? Which differences did you observe when singing during the planet's day hour versus its night hour? If you worked with multiple planets, what differences did you observe?

✴

Sealing the Vessel with Joy

I came to this realization while working in vision out in the stars. I was out in the stars, drifting among the planets, when I heard a series of sounds. Each of the planets have their own 'sound' or vibration, and I was amazed to listen to this 'choir' as I drifted.

– Josephine McCarthy[17]

I N THE PREVIOUS TWO EXERCISES you gained access to some of the most powerful techniques that our ancestors discovered for us: the skill of lighting your inner fire through the sound of your voice, and the skill of working the light of the seven planets. As you gain experience in combining and applying these skills, you'll come to realize how efficient and impactful they are. Most twentieth century planetary rituals look overly cumbersome once you have established your own practice of singing in planetary light. Just remember these two basic facts: Firstly, both the planet and you can produce sounds and melodies. Secondly, both the planet's body (made up of gas, rock, water, etc.) and yours (made up of flesh, bone, blood, etc.) are sources of a constantly modulating and cyclically returning pattern of light. In your visionary work with these skills, much of your practice will focus on effectively tuning into, combining, and separating the twin forces of sound and light, emitted from two beings (you and the planet) engaged in a celestial exchange.

Creating communion with your holy daimon might take extended periods of isolation. If this is not actually physical isolation, it will certainly be isolation in regard to the nature of your spiritual work. For this process to work effectively you should not discuss the details of it with others; at least not until you have managed to establish a sound initial connection with your holy daimon. The journey has to be undertaken in silence.

Emptying our vessel of sensory impressions is a process that can open us up to the experience of stillness and ultimately one-pointedness; it can also expose us more actively to those emotions we tend to avoid. In the

---

17 Josephine McCarthy, *Quareia: The Apprentice*, module 9, lesson 1.

process, sadness, loneliness, yearnings and cravings are experiences we must be ready to encounter and deal with.

The tools given to you in the previous chapters provide some essential help in tackling these situations constructively. Many of our potentially negative experiences in silence are rooted in the patterns of our individual personalities. From an astrological viewpoint, our personality is made from a living web of planetary influences and power dynamics. Singing in the light of the respective planets can become a powerful tool of counterbalancing and healing imbalanced aspects in our natal charts.

For communion with our holy daimon, we only need to expose ourselves to one particular planet, and that is the Sun. Return to your space of practice where you are undisturbed and your work cannot be overheard. Sit in a comfortable position. For this exercise you will not need anything with you. You must know where the Sun is at the time of your practice; to achieve the best possible results, you should practice during the morning hour of the Sun. You will use the (barbaric) words, psalm line, or sentence that enables you to tune into the Sun's light. Now, as you are sitting in your quiet space, settle yourself into a place of silence and presence with the meditation technique of your choice. As before, you can use one of the tratak techniques or the Meditation of the Void.

When the time is right and you are centred in silence, reach out to the celestial body of the Sun. Stretch your vision until you reach this burning, ever-exploding mass of gas and fire, and draw it down towards you. Again, do not attempt to control this process too much. And do not draw the Sun too close: the goal is to establish a space of shared presence between yourself and the Sun, not to become another Icarus.

A good outcome would be to have a vision the Sun before you on the horizon, perhaps slightly larger than normal. Much more important is the inner connection established between you and the Sun through the act of drawing it down. Begin to sing for the Sun, and at the same time tune yourself to be receptive to its answering sound. Concentrate your awareness on the midpoint between you and the Sun and tune your senses to pick up what is happening there. You could pick up information through any of your senses – sight, smell, touch, hearing, even taste.

Do not spend too much time at the focal point between your two energy patterns. Rather return to it often, and learn how to tune yourself into it even when you are not in vision. This is the place, outside of yourself, where you seal your vessel with joy. This sort of joy could not be further removed from the common emotional reaction to good fortune or good luck. This kind of joy is silent as the muttered prayer yet loud as the roar of the celestial lion. It is our mind and body radiating the vibration triggered by synchronizing our voice with the utterance of the Sun. This kind of joy is not an emotional response, but the experience of a natural force. Going too deeply into this joy will burn us up; and if we stray too far from it we will drown in sadness.

The planetary spirits are not all-knowing, all-powerful mummies and daddies who will spoon-feed you and answer every dumb question you can think to ask. Rather they are the mediators of forces that affect everything. They are intermediaries from whom you can seek guidance in relation to the influence they mediate. They do not care if you live or die, fail or succeed; they engage only when you are looking to work consciously with the power they mediate. They are the stepped-down voice of a very large chunk of rock and metal hurtling through space. Do not be tempted to put human ideals and emotions onto them (...). Learn to work with them as they are.[18]

✳

18 Josephine McCarthy, *Quareia: The Apprentice*, module 9, lesson 8

STAGE 3 · DARKNESS

Why Darkness Matters

We are about to enter the most daring and challenging stage of this path. As an introduction to the spirit of the work awaiting us, let us look at two pieces, the first is 'A Vision at Night,' an episode from *The Legend of the Baal-Shem*:

> The angel of the Lord seized me in the night and led me out, and I stood in the void, and the night weighed on my shoulders like a huge burden, and from below the night rolled onto me towards my soles. And the angel spoke: 'Behold!' and the darkness vanished and I stood effortlessly in a bright void and I beheld. There was a circle between two abysses. And in the area of the circle, a red abyss was engulfed like a lake of blood; and outside the area of the circle, a black abyss extended like an ocean of night. And I saw, behold!, a man was walking on the ridge like a blind man, with staggering feet, and his two weak hands touched upon the abysses to his right and to his left, and his chest was made from glass, and I beheld his heart fluttering like leaves in the wind, and on his forehead was the sign of the ice. And the man walked on and on, on the path formed by the ridge, without looking left or right, and he had almost reached the end of the circle which also marked its beginning. And I wanted to shout out to him, yet my gaze dazed my tongue. And suddenly the man lifted his view, and saw left and right, and stumbled, and from the two abysses, arms reached up to hold him. There the angel touched my lips, and my tongue was released, and I called and cried out to that man: 'Raise your wings and fly!' And lo, the human raised his wings, and no weakness or stupor was any longer about him, and the ridge disappeared from underneath his feet, and the abyss of blood was devoured by God's reservoirs of water and the abyss of the night vanished in God's light, and the city of God was there, open to all sides.

The second piece to consider is a poem by Rainer Maria Rilke:

The Panther

His vision, from the constantly passing bars,
has grown so weary that it cannot hold
anything else. It seems to him there are
a thousand bars; and behind the bars, no world.

As he paces in cramped circles, over and over,
the movement of his powerful soft strides
is like a ritual dance around a center
in which a mighty will stands paralyzed.

Only at times, the curtain of the pupils
lifts, quietly—. An image enters in,
rushes down through the tensed, arrested muscles,
plunges into the heart and is gone.

Now, as different as these two accounts seem, they both convey a picture
of a being caught in a pattern of suffering: here the man walking on the
ridge of the lake of blood, there the panther in its cage, trapped behind
metal bars. Before we dare throw ourselves headlong into the stage of
Darkness, we should undertake a quick mental exercise: What would
it take for you, despite their obvious states of suffering, to nonetheless
imagine both panther and man as happy beings? You can also work the
experiment in reverse. Consider the panther freed from its cage and the
man elevated by mysterious wings: can you still imagine them as unhappy?

Darkness is the stage in which we prepare ourselves to be ripped out of
the habitual patterns we have created for ourselves. It is the stage in which
we prepare ourselves to make a commitment to the universe; the commitment that we are ready to let go.

The problem with such a commitment is that whatever will be taken
from us, whatever we will be forced to let go off, might still seem better
in retrospect than what we receive in return. To the panther at least its
enemies are nearby and clearly known: the metal bars of its cage and the
human that holds the key. The same goes for the man on the ridge, his

heart might be trembling, yet his steps are predictable, bound to the circumference of the lake of blood.

Every painful situation, as much as it costs, also affords us some sort of (indirect) gain. Clinically such gains are called 'secondary gains.' A seconary gain might present itself as an illness or a stroke of bad luck which actually shields us from performing certain tasks, from carrying out certain responsibilities, or from having to fulfil certain social demands. Looked at in bright daylight such 'deals' might seem cynical at best, yet they do provide some sort of positive return on their unpleasant investments.

What are the deals we have locked ourselves into? Would we be willing, together with the pain they inflict, to give up all the gains we make from them? We might be caged like the panther, muscles atrophied behind the metal bars but at least there is regular food and no need to worry about bigger panthers. Or our hearts might be trembling and our hands might be weak like the man walking the ridge around the lake of blood but at least following our own footsteps makes for a familiar path. Whatever the scale of our suffering, repeating the same patterns of pain again and again makes for a damn fine predictable rhythm.

Few of us truly know how much we have to lose, or how much we take for granted. To walk consciously into darkness, lead by nothing but one's free will, is no mean feat. Like most of man's great adventures, it balances on that fine edge between courageous boldness and reckless stupidity.

So before we proceed, you might want to take a moment to give thanks for everything you have received. Think about your situation right now, of all the things you risk taking for granted. Look at them before they disappear in darkness, and acknowledge your thankfulness for their presence. Look especially upon the things you haven't noticed for a long time with thankfulness. What do you learn from them about your present situation? Can you see how they form your circle of blood? Are you fully prepared to be lifted away from them?

Here are my personal words after acknowledging my situation:

How much grace is in my limitations! I am graced by being bound into this present time. I need to only think about the here and now; not my father's sins, not my grandfather's sins. I am graced by being bound into this present body. I need to only feel the here and now; whatever reaches towards me, whatever I am reaching towards, right here, right now. I am graced by being bound into this present place. I need to only see the here and now. I see this place, this night, this moon; I do not see my mother's night, I do not see my grandmother's moon. Blessed be my boundaries.

Whether it is the darkness of cosmic space, the darkness of the womb, or the darkness of the grave, it is in darkness where all new life is born and to which it returns. Darkness is the realm in which one can no longer uphold one's own boundaries. It is the place where 'other' and 'us' bleed into one. Since time immemorial, darkness has swallowed whole the dream of human sovereignty. Since the first dying fire in our ancestor's cave, darkness has been the boundless home of all our demons and fears.

On our journey towards communion with our holy daimon we have already experienced the powers of trust and joy. There is one more pearl to add to this string, and that is courage. Courage is often misunderstood as the blunt boldness that is the apparently natural gift of those few who seem immune from the fear and angst that binds the rest of us. The reality could not be more different.

Courage, at least the kind that will support us magically, cannot exist without the profound firsthand experience of its shape-shifting black twin, the one that we call fear. To deliberately develop such courage we have to make a conscious decision, and that is to walk up to our fears and look them straight in the eye. To stand calmly, face to face with everything our instincts tell us to hide from, to run from, to avoid, and to abhor. It is a decision to overcome our inborn instinct against acknowledging our own darkness.

What follows is a raw experience: the experience of still being able to stand up, despite everything we have lost. Despite everything that threatens what we have left, despite all that devalues us, that fills us with shame, that makes our heart sink, our throats tighten, our teeth chatter. Out of this painful experience comes a new kind of courage, a courage born from the knowledge that despite all that has happened, we can co-exist with this darkness and still be fine. Standing naked like this before the mirror of our fears, we see our true form. Most of us will see that form a little differently than we expected, but we are still here, nonetheless. And having beheld that vision, having ceased to evade it, we can then start to change it.

As adept magicians, much of our work consists of preparing for our own death while we are living, so that we can die skilfully when the time comes. In that way we can walk out of death and into another life gracefully and with as much wisdom, gentleness, and forgiveness towards ourselves and others as possible. That is how creation purifies itself, by us purifying ourselves from one death to another. It is a cycle that spans centuries, millennia even. A cycle of lives and deaths, woven by fate, and watched over by our holy daimon as the protector of the spark that we are, as it walks out into creation and returns from it.

So how could facing the mirror of our fears and standing in darkness possibly hurt us more than we can bear? We have done nothing that has not been done before, we have told no lie that has not been told before, and we have neither suffered nor caused any newborn evil to enter this world on our watch. None of our lives are new births; no evil scar, no lying song, no tearful eye is altogether new. The newness of our lives lies not in their raw materials, but in what we choose to make of them; not in our experiences, but in our reactions to them. We are judged not by our unethical thoughts, by our amoral feelings, or by our opinion of our self worth. We are judged by our deeds.

This third stage is called Darkness, not courage, because to learn a new skill we must focus on the necessary work before us, not on what we hope to gain from it. And what we have to work on is our exposure to, our resilience to, and our ease with, the reality of our own darkness. Because it is absolutely impossible for our holy daimon to talk to us in a manner that we can consciously apprehend while we choose to hide behind a mask, armour, or second skin.

Exercises in Darkness

Standing at the threshold

If every Initiate would only attend to his own development before
seeking to perform all sorts of activities far beyond his capabilities, the
Mysteries would be much more effective among humans than they are
at present. Good intentions are insufficient substitutes for good sense.

– W. G. Gray

This exercise brings you to a threshold from which, having crossed over
it, you cannot return. For it you will need a lightproof and ideally soundproof space. I used a small walk-in cupboard. As a last resort, you could
use a sleeping mask to create a virtual black space. Learn the following
incantation by heart:

*Take what is worn. Devour what is waste. Peruse what is I. For I am not afraid, but
born from your fire. We will meet again and again. In your crucible of ashes and life.*

At the morning or night hour of Saturn, sit with a lit candle before you
and ground yourself in silence and presence, then perform the Meditation
of the Void. When you are in the centre of the flame and you can feel the
void surrounding you, carefully lean forward. Then, at the same time as
you blow out the candle, see the central flame vanish in vision. Now sit
centred in the void, in a space that no longer has a centre.

When you have grown accustomed to the darkness, reach out towards
the eastern horizon. Let your mind reach further into the void of the
East, in a straight line, deeper and deeper into the vast horizon. Reach
out until your vision finds the sphere of Saturn. Far ahead, emerging
out of darkness, you can see the Old One who never speaks yet always
listens. Settle back into stillness as you watch the outline of Saturn. There
is nothing in this world now, only the void, Saturn, your vision, and the
distance between you.

Now begin to sing for Saturn, the fearmonger. Sing to the planet and
sing to the consciousness from which it is built. Sing to this ancient

being, caught in a body of rock and gas and celestial rings. Sing to Saturn who has both formed and destroyed every single human being, and who now stands before you.

Take what is worn. Devour what is waste. Peruse what is I. For I am not afraid, but born from your fire. We will meet again and again. In your crucible of ashes and life.

When you are done, fall back into silence and observe what is happening right here, right now. When you are ready, return to the flame in vision. (You need not light the physical candle.) Just as you reached out to Saturn before, reach out to the flame and let yourself be pulled back into it. Stay in the flame and keep your vision in the flame's bright, cleansing light. Then return to your body. With open eyes, sit in darkness awhile.

Write down your observations and insights in your magical diary. You might find it helpful to reflect on the following questions: What happened before you began singing, and how did it change when you sang? What prompted you to end the exercise? Before you entered the flame again, what do you remember? In the hours following your Saturn practice, what thoughts arose, which ideas formed? What did these thoughts or ideas reveal to you about your current relationship with Saturn?

Spend anything from a few weeks to a few years on this exercise. The celestial cycle of Saturn lasts twenty-seven years; this gives you an impression of this planet's slow rhythm and the kind of changes you have initiated in yourself. In our short lives we only go through a few cycles like these. Do this exercise no more than thirteen times. Do not deliberately force yourself to initiate or change anything in your life; quite the opposite. Perhaps perform the exercise every Saturday morning and evening at Saturn's planetary hour. Then spend the rest of the week observing, taking the world in, and being gentle with yourself. Don't forget: you are being worked on now. Changes will manifest themselves in their own time; do not be afraid to follow your instincts, for it will be your instincts that will change first.

Crossing the threshold

Because where you begin, you will also need to end.

– *Abramelin*, Book 3, chapter 2, §.209.

OUR TRADITION includes many different techniques for deriving our holy daimon's name from our birth chart. In truth, our holy daimon will not care too much about what name we assign her/him. But she/he will care tremendously about what we do with this name – a name that only we should know. For now, you need to obtain your natal chart. Another possibilty is to use the time of your conception, if your parents remember!

As this process involves a series of rather specific astrological calculations, I have made an Excel spreadsheet which is available for free on my website.[19] You should be careful to use the correct tab on the Excel sheet for your calculation, the first tab, called 'Daytime' if your birth was during the day, and the second tab, 'Nighttime' if it was at night. Or you can make the calculation yourself. The method is detailed in chapter twenty-six of Agrippa's *Fourth Book of Occult Philosophy*.

Once you have the name, write the following incantation from the Greek magical papyri in your magical diary, putting the name of your holy daimon in place of N.N. Then learn the short incantation by heart:

For you are I and I am you; your name is mine, and mine is yours. For I am your image, N.N.[20]

Now return to your lightproof, soundproof space, get into your preferred meditation posture, and settle into the presence and silence. You can use the *tratak* exercises given previously. When you are calm and centred, close your eyes and perform the Meditation of the Void. When you are fully settled in the flame, and entirely surrounded by the void, extinguish the light in your vision. Float in darkness for a while. Stay present in the

---

19 https://theomagica.com/tools.
20 PGM, in Betz, The Delphic Maxim 'Know Yourself.'

ocean of darkness, in the absence of everything around you, then begin to sing the incantation of your holy daimon. Do not sing it expecting your holy daimon to appear, rather, expect her/him to hear you.

Sing in devotion. Continue to sing towards the presence of your holy daimon. It may take a while. Expect your holy daimon to be surprised when she/he begins to hear your song, because for the first time in your life, you are no longer singing to the mirror, but you have turned around and started singing to the real thing. Keep on singing. You do not need instructions on how to follow up on this practice. You will know by now.

Reflections on Darkness

> Some say that doing philosophy began with the barbarians.
> – Diogenes Laërtius[21]

HANS-DIETER BETZ remarked that the link between the Delphic maxim 'Know yourself' and the Greek magical papyri (PGM) is far more complex than a simple footnote.[22] Indeed, the relationship between one of the most famous ancient Greek maxims and one of the oldest collections of Western magical texts is very hard to unravel. At the heart of the matter is the question faced at some point by everyone interested in the PGM, which is whether the corpus is one of ritualized philosophy or philosophized ritual. Which came first, the magical act or the philosophical notion? Was magic a way of validating a map that had already been worked out theoretically by philosophers, or was the map drawn on the basis of magically acquired data? Did the best magicians develop into philosophers, or did the most daring philosophers develop into magicians? Above all this stands Socrates' discussion of the maxim 'Know yourself' in Plato's *Alcibiades Maior*.[23] Here, according to Plato's account, Socrates questions what the self really is that we are encouraged to know. His an-

---

21 Diogenes Laërtius, 1.1, in Copenhaver, 88.
22 Betz (1981), 156.
23 Betz (1981), 157.

swer ends with a few pithy statements which have profoundly influenced the concept of self-control and self-knowledge in the West:

> 'So the human being is an entity different from his own body.' 'Then what is the human being?' 'The soul is the human being.' 'Then the god who instructs us to know ourselves orders us to know the soul.'[24]

The magicians behind the Greek magical papyri interpreted Socrates' words quite differently from the philosophers. Generations of philosophers took Socrates' words as an exhortation to deep philosophical self examination. The magicians took it as an exhortation to conjure the holy daimon. Both responses were attempts to resolve the same paradox. If the physical world is a theatre of illusion under whose spell we are born, live and die, then how can we free ourselves from it without outside help? Socrates, in Plato's *Alcibiades Maior*, slightly alters the Delphic maxim to better illustrate this paradox and its philosophical consequences. Instead of saying to a human 'know thyself,' he commands an eye to 'see itself.' Let us read the relevant section in full:

SOCRATES: I will tell you what I suspect to be the real advice which the inscription [of the Delphic Maxim] gives us. I rather think there are not many illustrations of it to be found, but only in the case of sight.
ALCIBIADES: What do you mean by that?
SOCRATES: Consider in your turn: suppose that, instead of speaking to a man, it said to the eye of one of us, as a piece of advice 'See thyself,' how should we apprehend the meaning of the admonition? Would it not be, that the eye should look at that by looking at which it would see itself?
ALCIBIADES: Clearly.
SOCRATES: Then let us think what object there is anywhere, by looking at which we can see both it and ourselves.
ALCIBIADES: Why, clearly, Socrates, mirrors and things of that sort.
SOCRATES: Quite right. And there is also something of that sort in the eye that we see with?

24 Plato, *Alcibiades Maior* 1.129e, 130c, 130e, in Betz (1981), 157.

ALCIBIADES: To be sure.

SOCRATES: And have you observed that the face of the person who looks
   into another's eye is shown in the optic confronting him, as in a mirror,
   and we call this the pupil, for in a sort it is an image of the person
   looking?

ALCIBIADES: That is true.

SOCRATES: Then an eye viewing another eye, and looking at the most
   perfect part of it, the thing wherewith it sees, will thus see itself.

ALCIBIADES: Apparently.

SOCRATES: But if it looks at any other thing in man or at anything in
   nature but what resembles this, it will not see itself.

ALCIBIADES: That is true.

SOCRATES: Then if an eye is to see itself, it must look at an eye, and at
   that region of the eye in which the virtue of an eye is found to occur;
   and this, I presume, is sight.

ALCIBIADES: That is so.

SOCRATES: And if the soul too, my dear Alcibiades, is to know herself,
   she must surely look at a soul, and especially at that region of it in
   which occurs the virtue of a soul – wisdom, and at any other part of a
   soul which resembles this?

ALCIBIADES: I agree, Socrates.

SOCRATES: And can we find any part of the soul that we can call more
   divine than this, which is the seat of knowledge and thought?

ALCIBIADES: We cannot.

SOCRATES: Then this part of her resembles God, and whoever looks at
   this, and comes to know all that is divine, will gain thereby the best
   knowledge of himself.[25]

So this is the escape route that Socrates lays out for us. In the theatre of
illusion in which we are all caught, there is only one way out: gaining true
knowledge of our selves. What breaks the spell of the mirror (the world
around us) is to turn away from it and instead look deeply into the wide
open eyes of the person next to us, that we might see ourselves in the re-

25 Plato, *Alcibiades Maior* 132d–133c, from *Plato in Twelve Volumes*, Vol. 8.

flection. This is the metaphorical answer to the Delphic maxim. But how do we apply it in practice?

Once again we receive guidance from Socrates' dialogue with Alcibiades. We must search within the soul for its most divine part, the part that is the seat of all knowledge and thought. Identifying the seat of knowledge was surprisingly straightforward for an ancient Greek magician, as the most divine part of the soul was a divine being in its own right; it was one's personal daimon.

> Once the equation of the self with the soul and the deity was made, another equation offered itself almost necessarily. The older concept of the soul as daimon had become highly important in the Socratic and Platonic traditions of thought, especially because of its connection with the so-called *Daimonion* of Socrates.[26]

Thus for the PGM magicians, knowledge of one's self was not to be gained through speculative thinking or scientific extrapolation, but by gaining sensual access to the being that encapsulated the essence of one's self. The logic implied in Socrates' explanation was not one of speculative self-examination, but one of 'oracular enquiry and reply.'[27] For the magicians, Socrates' instruction was no philosophical metaphor, but a gnostic method.

We have evidence that such 'oracular interpretation'[28] goes back at least to the first century CE. In the writings of the Stoic philosopher Epictetus we find an interesting and somewhat more pragmatic version of the Delphic maxim:

> Take council very carefully, know yourself, consult your personal daimon, without God undertake nothing.[29]

---

26 Betz (1981), 158.
27 Betz (1981), 159, ref. also 171.
28 Betz (1981), 159.
29 Epictetus, Diss.III.22.53, in Betz (1981), 159.

Amongst the vast corpus of the Greek magical papyri we find several references to working with one's holy daimon and a specific rite detailed in PGM VII.505–528. In the following, final chapter we will use a restored version of this gnostic ritual to initiate the final stage of our work. However, we should also mention that we have already integrated and activated an alternative technique, which is also given in the magical papyri, for achieving divine union, in the previous exercise.

> For you are I, and I am you; your name is mine, and mine is yours. For I am your image.[30]

In the Greek magical papyri, the above invocation is directed at Hermes as the highest god. However, this is a widespread ancient formula of identification, and versions of it – and especially of its opening line – are found throughout both occidental and oriental mystical traditions. In his 1919 study on the history of prayer titled *Das Gebt*, Friedrich Heiler (1892–1967) brilliantly demonstrated this mystical prayer's ubiquity, and provided Indian, Hellenistic, Gnostic and Sufi versions of it.[31] This 'formula of reciprocal identity'[32] between the practitioner and the divine was what Heiler viewed as the highest form of mystical experience.

> The mystics form an invisible brotherhood ranging over all countries and times; separated by miles of distance and centuries of years, they reach for each others' hands and join the choir: man and god are separated only by outer appearance, both are in unresolvable union. And in drunken passion they utter the great mystical prayer: 'I am you and you are I.'[33]

Letting another spiritual being dwell within us, whether a god-form or our holy daimon, can indeed be considered the highest goal of mystical union. But it can equally be interpreted as the expulsion of our mortal selves.

30 PGM VIII, lines 36–38.
31 Heiler, 306.
32 Heiler, 306.
33 Heiler, 307.

Are we really deifying ourselves when we invite the divine to dwell within us? Or are we in fact extinguishing our mortal selves (and materializing the divine), by offering ourselves up as an empty vessel? To the ancient monastic mystic this question would not have mattered. But it might matter to those of us with everyday lives to lead, families to support, and other mundane traits that we are not ready to give up. When we say 'For you are I, and I am you,' we are consenting to be lifted away from the lake of blood, to be broken out of our cage. You have come a long way. Now be careful with your choices. Singing these lines to Saturn is an invitation to enter darkness, a darkness equally required for the growth of our divine seed and for dissolving what constrains it.

Like the fluidum of a god flows into his statue, in order to take its effect there as the living divine I, so it also flows into the body of the initiate.[34]

*

---

34 Betz (1981), 166.

STAGE 4 · ENCOUNTER

Systasis with your personal daimon

Strive on indeed, and be sure that it is not you that is mortal, but
only your body. For that man whom your outward form reveals is not
yourself; the Daimon is the true self, not that physical figure that can
be pointed out by the finger. Know, then, that you are a god, if a god is
that which lives, feels, remembers and foresees, and which rules, governs and moves the body over which it is set, just as the supreme God
above us rules the universe.

– Cicero, *De re publica*, 6.24.26

NTERING CONSCIOUS COMMUNION with our holy daimon is the
result of a successful process of inner alchemy. Any methods to induce
such a process are but a catalyst for something that nature is perfectly
capable of achieving on her own terms. Nature creates gold, however,
it requires a very specific set of circumstances and actively involved
forces.

As magicians we have a dual function in this process: we are both active
agents and passive recipients. To achieve communion with our personal
daimon we work upon ourselves. We are the substance to be transformed
and one of several forces necessary to achieve this transformation. In
working such alchemy on ourselves, it is critical to balance our active
agency with our passive absorption, allowing our spiritual body to be activated while aiding the process by assuming the right posture and presence
at the right moment. It is important to remember that it is when we as
magicians are quiet and seemingly passive that the spirits become most
active. It is precisely during the state of our silent absorption that we find
our daimon working most actively upon us.

When the atmosphere is charged sufficiently with electricity, it dis-
charges as lightning. Just because we haven't seen any lightning yet, we
cannot assume that nothing is happening. Producing a thin vein of gold
takes millennia within the natural setting of subterranean rock. Spending
a few years or an entire decade on achieving conscious communion with

our holy daimon is an incredibly accelerated timeline by mother nature's standards. The ritual instructions are intended to induce, not shortcut, a natural spiritual process.

The main body of this ritual stems from the third or fourth century CE, and is taken from PGM VII.505–528. While the brief ritual has been analysed by several academic scholars, it has not, so far, gained the attention of practicing magicians. Here I will suggest a way of applying it to a practical rite of visionary ritual magic.

Before we explore the practice of PGM VII.505, note that we are assuming that the original text was left intentionally ambiguous. The following detailed instructions are one of many possible ways of activating the dormant magical patterns in the text. We want to encourage readers to develop their own practical versions of this rite. However, any adjustments or alterations should not be based on personal preference or theoretical speculation, but on firsthand experience of what practically yields the best results.

In Part II, I shared my path for achieving communion with my holy daimon. It has value for other practitioners in two main ways. First, it offers evidence that such processes are still achievable today. I hope my own account will serve as spiritual encouragement, if it is needed. Second, and more importantly, my personal account shows how this particular spiritual encounter unfolded for me, before I came across the PGM ritual.

During the night of contact, my holy daimon took me through a series of experiences in quick succession. In retrospect I'd describe them as alchemical reactions. They were very intense physically and spiritually, and at the time I had no idea what was happening to me.

Many years later I came across PGM VII.505 and the ritual process of 'skinning' the magician of several spirits that normally interfere with the perception of everyday reality. The parallels with my own experience were immediately striking. In fact, they helped me better understand the purpose of a ritual that my holy daimon had since instructed me to perform, at least once a month, without any explanation. As so often in magic, the spirits do not care whether we understand what we do, only that we do it right.

Sharing these ritual instructions is the closing of a circle of almost twenty years of spiritual study and work. I should mention that as I had already established communion with my holy daimon by the time I came across PGM VII.505, I cannot confirm how this rite will work for someone at a different stage in their alchemical process. I can attest, however, to its impact on my own practice, and how incredibly coherent it is with aspects of inner alchemy that are not normally spoken about in the Western tradition.

Finally, before we proceed to the ritual, we should establish a shared understanding of how our ancestors worked these kinds of rites. What is critical to highlight, and what is most often overlooked, is the difference between orthodoxy and orthopraxy.

✶

Understanding Orthopraxy

THE TERM ORTHOPRAXY stands in direct opposition to today's more familiar term orthodoxy. The latter means 'correct belief,' the former 'correct practice.' Our Egyptian and Greek ancestors were deeply concerned about orthopraxy, and could not have cared less about orthodoxy. Now let us explore why that was the case. ¶ For our ancient ancestors, the spiritual realm with all its inhabitants was an everyday reality that was experienced directly, firsthand. How people thought about spiritual beings or whether or not they believed in them simply wasn't a relevant question. Let us go to a present day example for comparison: we would never ask whether someone believes in computers, electricity, or even virtual reality. We experience all three of them every day: for us they are a matter of firsthand knowledge, not faith. As far as this example is concerned, we are concerned with correct practice: we could not care less about correct belief. Our ancestors were exactly the same in regard to the spiritual realm.

A strict translation of the Greek ὀρθοδοξία (*orthodoxia*) is 'right opinion.' Opinions did not matter in a world that required continuous magical action: acts to guard the forces of the underworld, acts to balance the tides and rivers, acts to sway life-weaving forces, acts to extract oracles from the guardians of fate, to name just a few.

Our ancient ancestors most likely did not care much about what people believed so long as they performed the correct ritual acts. However, unlike modern academics, adepts in the ancient world would have certainly taken great care to coordinate the inner and outer performance of their rituals. That is, aligning and combining acts of magic performed in vision with acts of magic performed with their physical bodies.

Orthopraxy in our present context, therefore, needs to be understood as concern over the 'correct practice' in both the inner and outer realms. The synchronization of these two is the goal of the following rite.

Ritual for systasis with your holy daimon

PGM VII.505

Meeting with your own daimon: 'Welcome, Tyche, and you daimon of this place, and you, the present hour, and you, the present day – and every day as well. Welcome, All-embracing, that is, earth and heaven. Welcome, Helios, for you are the one who has established yourself in invisible light over the holy firmament ORKORĒTHARA. You are the father of the reborn Aion ZARACHTHŌ; you are the father of the in-accessible Nature Thortchophanō; you are the one who has in yourself the mixture of universal nature and who begot the five wandering stars, which are the entrails of heaven, the guts of earth, the fountainhead of

174

the waters, and the courage of fire AZAMACHAR ANAPHANDAŌ EREYA ANEREYA PHENPHENSŌ IGRAA; you are the youthful one, highborn, scion of the holy temple, kinsman to the holy mere called Abyss which is located beside the two pedestals SKIATHI and MANTŌ. And the earth's four foundations were shaken, O master of all, holy Scarab, AŌ SATHREN ABRASAX IAŌAI AEŌ ĒOA ŌAĒ IAO IĒO EY IE IAŌAI.' Write the name in myrrh ink on two male eggs. You are to cleanse yourself thoroughly with one; then lick off the name, break it, and throw it away. Hold the other in your partially open right hand and show it to the sun at dawn and (crowned with) olive branches; raise up your right hand, supporting the elbow with your left hand. Then speak the formula seven times, crack the egg open, and swallow its contents. Do this for seven days, and recite the formula at sunset as well as sunrise.

The restored inner and outer performance of PGM VII.505:

WHAT YOU WILL NEED FOR THIS RITE

- A quiet, undisturbed place where you can speak without being overheard.
- A candle and matches.
- Six pebbles, the size of an egg, not used in any previous magical acts.
- Two fresh, washed, organic, raw eggs.
- A water-soluble ink that is safe to ingest, ideally made from pure myrrh.
- A fine brush.
- The location of the Sun at the time of the rite.
- Sufficient commitment to repeat this rite ideally twice a day at dusk and dawn for several weeks.

PREPARING THE EGGS

Prepare the ink and use the brush to write the following divine name on both eggs. Start at the base or top of the egg and coil the text around the shell:

'AŌ SATHREN ABRASAX IAŌAI AEŌ ĒOA ŌAĒ IAO IĒO EY IE IAŌAI'

Ritual to induce a meeting with your Holy Guardian Angel

ETURN TO THE QUIET, undisturbed place where you cannot be overheard. Sit in a comfortable position. Taking the six stones you brought with you, place three to your left and three to your right. Place the two eggs behind you. All the items must be within reach without your needing to move about much. Finally, light the candle and place it in front of you.

As in the previous exercises, ground yourself in silence and presence and perform the Meditation of the Void. Once you are surrounded by darkness, abide in it awhile, then step through the void and once more take up position in your resting physical body.

Pick up the first stone. Quietly keep it in your hands until it is the same temperature as your body, then begin to roll it between your palms. In vision, see how with each turn of the stone you are drawing off some of your own skin and working it into the stone. When you have worked an entire layer of your skin into the stone, hold it still in the womb of your hands, breathe into it, and say, 'Welcome, Tyche, spirit of fate.' Place it in front of you, behind the invisible line marked by the candle flame.

Now pick up the second stone. Repeat the process above. When you have taken off another layer of your skin in vision, hold the stone still between your palms and say, 'And welcome to you, daimon of this place.'

Pick up the third stone and repeat the process again. When you have taken another layer from your body and are sitting in stillness, say, 'And welcome to you, daimon of the present hour.'

Now pick up the stones from your other side, one by one. Repeat the process, and speak as follows:

· With the fourth: *And welcome to you, daimon of the present day.*
· With the fifth: *And welcome to you, daimon of time and every day.*
· With the sixth: *And welcome to you, daimon of the All-embracing, that is, earth and heaven.*

Keep your eyes open or closed, as you prefer, and sit for a moment in the presence of the six daimons you have called forth. Whatever your visionary sensual preferences are, ensure that you are in touch with each of them as they are represented by the physical substance of the stones in front of you. Perhaps your magical body will see them in vision as they rest in front of you bound into the stones. Maybe your magical body will hear them in vision or perceive slightly different astral smells or melodies. Do not force it, simply sit and feel the connection between you and the six spirits, however it manifests.

Now take the first egg and carefully stroke it over your body. Without cracking its shell, rub yourself with the egg as if it was a sponge. This will draw out any residue left by the six spirits whom you have already called forth. Cleanse yourself carefully with the egg. When you are done, lick off the divine name written on it, crack it open and empty it onto the ground between you, the candle, and the six stones. Observe in vision how the residue taken off by the egg is now picked up by each of the six spirits. No life force remains in the egg or its shell.

You now sit skinned and purified before the candle. Inspect your body in vision, how it looks, and how the absence of your six normal skins (fate, place, hour, day, time, sublunary realm) has affected and changed it.

Take the second egg. Centre yourself again in the void and, as you have done before, reach out for the Sun. Push further and further into the dark until you draw close to that vast celestial body. As we have said before, do not get too close to the Sun, especially now that you are without your six skins. Just as with your earlier work with planetary light, nothing exists now except for you, the Sun, and the distance between you. Do not rush this part of the ritual, take your time to establish good contact. Reach for the Sun's light and pull some of its cosmic fire into the egg in your hands. You can do this with your hands in vision or, if you prefer, through sound and song. Continue to fill the egg with fire until it is warm in your palms. In vision you will see how it begins to glow, like a burning ember held in your hands full of cosmic fire. Then raise your right hand, supporting your elbow with your left hand, with the egg in your palm, and speak these words:

Welcome, Helios, for you are the one who has established yourself in invisible light over the holy firmament ORKORĒTHARA. You are the father of the reborn Aion ZARACHTHŌ; you are the father of the inaccessible Nature Thortchophanō; you are the one who has in yourself the mixture of universal nature and who begot the five wandering stars, which are the entrails of heaven, the guts of earth, the fountainhead of the waters, and the courage of fire AZAMACHAR ANAPHANDAŌ EREYA ANEREYA PHENPHENSŌ IGRAA; you are the youthful one, highborn, scion of the holy temple, kinsman to the holy mere called Abyss which is located beside the two pedestals SKIATHI and MANTŌ. And the earth's four foundations were shaken, O master of all, holy Scarab, AŌ SATHREN ABRASAX IAŌAI AEŌ ĒOA ŌAĒ IAO IĒO EY IE IAŌAI.

You can speak the formula up to seven times. Make sure, however, that you know it by heart. Repeat it until its rhythm fills your whole mind and the sacred space around you. Then crack open the egg and swallow its contents. In vision, follow the cosmic fire bound into the egg as it travels into your body. Observe how it affects you. What you now see are pure, divine forces at play, preparing your spiritual body for the touch of your holy daimon. Do not interfere with this process, do not touch it with your mortal wishes or imagination. Just be present while the cosmic fire spreads through your body.

Now you have become the vessel into which your holy daimon can descend. For as long as you wish, sit in silent presence and observe the space around you. When you are ready, call for your holy daimon. Normally it is enough to sing the name of your daimon. Realize that the burning body of the Sun is still before you, its solar wind brushing over your purified body, as you sing to call your holy daimon.

Finally, in whatever shape or geometric form it assumes, visualize your holy daimon approach you from behind. It is vast and beautiful. Take all the time you need to realize its presence. Then see how it is reaching out for you. It is now touching you on your shoulders. Everything else will transpire naturally. You are now in holy communion.

Interpretation

The ritual can be divided into five stages. In practice these stages may well blur and blend, but in order that we understand the underlying spiritual process clearly, we'll examine them in turn. Note that we will not discuss the fifth stage, the communion with your holy daimon, as this happens in vision alone.

STAGE 1: SKINNING

The first stage consists of welcoming six spiritual beings who normally remain indistinguishable from our everyday reality, too close to us to be seen. We tend to forget about these 'skins' of fate, space, and time.
The first part of this ritual peels back these layers of our skin and changes them from inherent aspects of our subjective experience into objective, spiritual counterparts so that we can begin to see them for what they truly are. This 'peeling back' is accomplished through a combination of inner vision and outer ritual as the magician welcomes and calls forth these spirits to stand beside them. We must recognize them for what they are: spirits in their own right, each with a unique spiritual essence. As they are already here, no complex rituals are needed, simply the spoken acknowledgement that they are present with us. By welcoming these spirits, the magician stops identifying with them:

Be welcome Tyche and you, Daimon of this place, and you, the present hour, and you the present day – and every day as well.

Now they stand next to us, bound in their own shapes and forms. We can see the weavers of life: the spirits of fate (Tyche), of the place, of the hour, of the day, and of the time. Imagine that your life is a play that lifts its curtain when you are born and lets it fall again when you return to the grave. The five spirit forces we just called forth provide everything required to put on that play:

- Fate (Tyche) = the plot.
- The spirit of the place = the stage and its actors.

- The spirits of the hour and day = the tone and the quality.
- The spirit of the time = the era and the setting.

We take one more step and call forth the spirit of the whole sublunary sphere:

Welcome, All-embracing, that is, earth and heaven.[35]

To return to the play analogy, having distanced ourselves from the stage, its settings, the other actors, and the plot, we now leave the building entirely. Doing so requires that the magician hold six unique spirit relationships in his mind: the spirits of his fate, the place, the hour, the day, the time, and the sublunary realm. Freeing ourselves from these skins means us giving them permission to go from being aspects of our individuality to once more being perceptible spirits in their own right. A magician who has proper command of their visionary skills will not have any problems accomplishing this. When invited to, the spirits will simply step forward from the body of the magician, and will present themselves in whatever forms are appropriate.

We use the physical anchors of six stones to identify and bind the six spirits. In principle this ritual could be done without those anchors. The stones, however, help a great deal. They let us involve our physical senses more deeply in the process, their substance provides homes for the spirits, and their round forms are ideal for the skins to coil around.

STAGE 2: PURIFYING
The second stage of the ritual is one of purification. To prepare for it, we wrote the divine name of Helios on two raw eggs, using either liquid myrrh or some other organic colour that can be licked off and ingested safely. As the name is relatively long, it will form several spirals round the egg: a wonderful reminder of the serpent and egg we encountered when we were building our trust.

---

35 My translation of Preisendanz's German rendering of PGM VII.509 (*Sei gegrüsst, Umfasendes, das ist Erde und Himmel*), as Betz's version is not so clear.

AŌ SATHREN ABRASAX IAŌAI AEŌ ĒŌA ŌAĒ IAO IĒO EY IE IAŌAI

Now we take the first of the two eggs and use it like a sponge over our whole body. We do not need to be naked for this, but thin, light clothing is preferable. Make sure you can feel the egg's pressure on your skin through the fabric, without risking breaking the egg accidentally.

The magical purpose of this stage is to ensure that our spiritual body is left completely clear and unblemished. When performed properly and by someone with sufficient magical skill, this stage is a very delicate process. It is a step further on from pulling the six skins from our body, which was already a sensitive matter. (Not because it was particularly hard, but because taking off these six skins has an enormous impact on our spiritual self; it is a major intervention into a process which is normally entirely self-regulated.)

The divine name written on the egg consecrates it to the cosmic force of creation, the spirit of which, in our present paradigm, is called Helios. This means the egg has become the active agent of a force so powerful that rarely reaches human beings unfiltered. Under normal conditions it is mediated and mitigated by several critical filters: the gate of the moon, the spirits of the sublunary realm (in particular the 360 genii of the zodiac), and finally the filters of time, day, hour, place, and fate, which are specific to each person. All these are the filters or skins we have just removed. Don't be fooled by the simplicity and straightforwardness of the act, using Helios to purify ourselves is quite the intervention. The use of the consecrated egg to extract the remaining residue can easily damage your spiritual pattern, which is why you licked off the divine name before you threw away the first egg. It was a safety measure to ensure that you actively reabsorb and take back any aspect of yourself that should remain within you.

STAGE 3: CHARGING

In the third stage we charge the second egg with cosmic fire pulled directly out of the sun. Little needs to be added to the instructions provided above. However, this stage does require good visionary skills, which is one reason why I had you practising the exercises to do with joy.

The formula to conjure Helios makes reference to many mythological concepts, some of which are Egyptian, others Greek. I recommend researching the meaning of each of these references thoroughly, some suggestions are to be found in the bibliography. As you'll be swallowing cosmic fire, you should know as much as possible about it beforehand. It will also help you appreciate the full beauty, richness, and depth of this ritual text. Here are some observations to help begin that process.

The original title of the PGM extract is *systasis idiou daimonos*. Various translations of this have been proposed, ranging from 'meeting with your personal daimon'[36] to 'communicating with your own daimon.'[37] Our attention should be drawn in particular to the word 'systasis.' We find the same word used in the Greek magical papyri in many rituals and spells to describe the relationship magicians aspire to create with other spirits, divinities, and even their *paredroi*. Early scholarly views about the word systasis tended to it being a literal meeting; later ones add more abstract connotations of connection and conjunction. As moderns, it is important to realize that for the ancient Greeks the term *systasis* was not a mystical term but a pragmatic, everyday word that described a meeting, whether this was a meeting between two people, or a person and a daimon.

Two other names in the conjuration deserve further attention, Skiathi and Mantō:

> You are the youthful one, highborn, scion of the holy temple, kinsman to the holy mere called Abyss which is located beside the two pedestals SKIATHI and MANTŌ.

Jan Bergman was the first scholar to provide a deep analysis of this important section of the ritual. The words *skiathi kai mantō* are the earliest known Greek transliterations of the two ancient Egyptian solar barks, (*Me*)*Sektet*, the Night Barque, and *Manedjet*, the Day Barque.[38] Even the sequence of naming the Night Barque before the Day Barque aligns with older Egyptian ritual texts such as *The Book of the Dead*. Also noteworthy

36 Pachoumi.
37 Bergman.
38 Bergman, 30.

is the word that comes before the two barques: 'pedestals' in the current translation. This likely refers to the floats on which models of such barques were placed for public rituals, though it could also be a translation error, in which case it should read 'boats.' The difficulty stems from the similarity between the Greek words *basis* and *baris*, the latter being a flat-bottomed Egyptian boat.[39]

Such a direct link between the magical papyri and an authentic Egyptian religious tradition is very rare; the author of this ritual knew exactly what they were doing. To better follow their line of thought, we recommend researching this lead further, paying particular attention to the god Khepri, often represented as a scarab beetle.

...for the Egyptian there was no form, no existence, no transformation, no coming into being without Khepri, the very prototype of birth and existence. This fundamental idea explains why exactly Khepri is chosen as the most effective god for our systasis-action.[40]

STAGE 4: INFLAMING

In the fourth and final stage of the rite the purified body is thoroughly embalmed and consecrated in cosmic fire. This fire has the potential to destroy as well as to create, it makes the ashes and the phoenix. It is not to be meddled with. Experiencing it was by far one of the most beautiful and breathtaking events of my life.

39 Bergman, 30.
40 Bergman, 32.

After you have performed this rite several times, you may start to notice significant changes to your spiritual body. Most of these are temporary and will last only for your systasis with your daimon. Remember again the analogy of the lightning. Just because it hasn't yet struck does not mean that no charge is building up. Have patience and confidence, and keep performing the rite. Results take time, not necessarily due to magical gestation, but because your spiritual senses have to sharpen.

Closing

I F YOU TAKE ONLY ONE THING from this book, I hope it will be how much you personally matter. You, as an ethical blueprint for all the wild spirits who admire us as beings of free-will. You, as a partner, student, teacher and co-creator with the myriad beings whom you'll encounter on the path. ¶ What does it mean to be you? And what would it take to be the best version of yourself? Aspiring to answer this question – every-day – is a journey of significant sacrifice and humility, of collaboration over competition, and of being willing to fail often and recover quickly. Yet, it is also a journey of unparalleled gifts and insights, of learning to ignite our own *hitlahavut* and seal our vessel in joy, of singing to ourselves and the light of the seven planets, and of separating ourselves from the daimones that normally bind us into body, time and space.

The gifts you'll receive and the sacrifices you'll be asked to make will differ on your own journey. There are many paths that lead to communion with your holy daimon. I hope you feel encouraged and empowered to follow your own path. And while traveling, let's remember that we are not alone, that complexity and sophistication are not the criteria that indicate effectiveness or efficacy in the art we are aspiring to master. The more we progress, the more we realize how little magic it takes to achieve true magic.

Our role in this journey is not to be the protagonist, but the substance that is acted upon. We are not the alchemist, but the powder in the flask. We are not the mason, but the raw stone in the quarry. Nature is the wisest being of all, and perfectly capable of bringing about communion with our holy daimon entirely by itself. All we need to do is to create the right conditions so that this process can happen right here, and right now.

May the art and the artist be united perfectly within us.

✳   ✳

✳

EPILOGUE

OR THIS EDITION OF HOLY DAIMON I would like to include a few thoughts that seem important to me since the first publication of the book in 2018. *Holy Daimon* remains the most intimate of my books to date. This is due to the excerpts from my magical diary which contain the most profound encounter with a daimon that I have experienced to date. However, it is not the contact itself, but the journey up to that point for which I will provide several essential way markers. As such, we have talked about Trust, Joy, and Darkness. If I were to write *Holy Daimon* again today, I might include one additional point, and I'd call it Longing.

Making conscious contact with one's daimon is, for most of us, an endeavour that takes years of work. In a world where young people have trouble sitting still to watch an entire feature film – let alone sit quietly for ninety minutes in asana – providing clarity about what this journey promises is essential.

I want to say a few words about why it is worthwhile to shed one's own preferences, habits, beliefs and eventually skins on the walk to our own burial. The encounter with our holy daimon is an incision that cuts into our lives. Regardless of the deep joy that this wound allows to flow into our lives, it still is a deep opening into everything we thought we were up until that point. Communion with our holy daimon will literally turn our bodies into light, and this will not happen without cutting us out of an imagined body which holds us back from this encounter.

Now, since this is an intimate book, and we've come to the end of it here, I want to talk about my own longings that drove me on this journey, and which I only now – in the rearview mirror of my own life – see with stinging clarity. Here, then, is an account of the ancestral body into which I was born.

In my family the following story is told about my great-grandfather, who was a well-known painter and graphic artist. Born in 1880, he spent his youth between Prague and Vienna and moved to Munich with his wife in 1908. In the years before the outbreak of the First World War he worked at the Munich Art Academy and was assigned to evaluate application portfolios. One day he came back from vacation and looked through the accumulated mail. Among them was a portfolio with the works of a young Austrian applicant, which appealed to him, and which he judged favourably. Unfortunately, the portfolio had been sent in too late or, due to his vacation, had now been viewed too late, so he sent the prospective artist a rejection letter. That artist's name was Adolf Hitler.

It is impossible to tell whether it happened exactly that way, but the fact is that Hitler applied twice unsuccessfully to the Vienna Art Academy and moved to Munich in 1913. Also a fact is that in the following years my great-grandfather became an active member and willing supporter of the Nazi Party, participated in both of the 'great' German art exhibitions at the Munich Haus der Kunst, was awarded the title of Professor on the Führer's birthday in 1938, and two years later received the Goethe Medal for Art and Science. In my family, Christmas cards with his kitschy mystical motifs are still sent out – seemingly fitting better with the family memory than his works *Tanks at the test site* (1941), *Defense against eastern incursions* (1943) or *SS Guards* (year unknown). I am not saying my great-grandfather was only a Nazi artist. But I am saying that nothing in his life mattered as much as his becoming a Nazi artist.

Paracelsus called necromancy a shadow art. We all grow up surrounded by the shadows of our ancestors, alive and dead. And just as shaded areas determine the growth of new plants, favouring certain species, stunting others, so our ancestors determine our own growth and inner landscapes as humans.

My ten year search for the holy daimon was driven by the naïve longing for a reference point outside the looming shadows of my ancestors. An anchor point that was untouched by the evil that I was born into. Deep inside, I was driven by the longing for an experience that, however temporarily, would allow me to shed the skin of my family history and clothe me in its daemonic presence. You can call such a desire escapist or existentialist, it really does not matter. Understanding the source of our longing for communion with our holy daimon is not a matter of judgement, but of acceptance.

I dedicate this book to all who share such a longing. Each one of us will have our own personal reasons. I share mine here to illustrate the point that more than a book about daemonic magic, this might really be a book about leading a good life, a life filled with joy and trust – though we still harbour flaws, depravity, or even evil, beneath our skin. In the best case, this could be a book about how to keep one's sanity, and heart, intact.

I hardly understand a word of what my holy daimon says to me. But when I asked my daimon, what lesson I can take from the story of my great-grandfather, s/he had a very simple answer: try not to be someone, try to be no one. For no ones stand together, whilst someones want to stand alone. No ones don't look at themselves, but at the work ahead. No ones can slip through the cracks of evil unseen, inspect it from within, learn from it while being touched by it, all the while quietly tending a plant in their own garden that absorbs evil.

✳   ✳

✳

SELECTED RESOURCES

CHALDEA

Butler, Elizabeth M. (1949). *Ritual Magic. Magic in History*. Cambridge: Cambridge University Press.

Carnoy, Albert (1912). Zoroastrianism. *Encyclopaedia of Religion and Ethics* Vol. 12. James Hastings (ed.). Edinburgh: T. & T. Clark; New York: C. Scribner's Sons.

Daicher, Samuel (1913). Babylonian Oil Magic in the Talmud and in the later Jewish Literature. London.

Horne, Charles Francis (1917). *The Sacred Books and Early Literature of the East*, Volume VII, Ancient Persia.

Lenormant, Francois (1877). *Chaldean Magic: Its Origin and Development*. London: Samuel Bagster.

Layard, Austen Henry (1849). *Nineveh and its Remains*, Vols. 1 & 2. London: John Murray.

Maspero, Gaston (1904). *History of Egypt, Chaldea, Syria, Babylonia and Assyria*, Vol.3. London: The Grolier Society.

Zimmern, Heinrich (1901). *Beiträge zur Babylonischen Religion*. Leipzig: J. C. Hinrichs.

ZOROASTRIANISM

Blois, Francois de (2000). Dualism in Iranian and Christian Traditions. *Journal of the Royal Asiatic Society* 10(1), 1–19.

Copenhaver, Brian P. (1992). *Hermetica: The Greek Corpus Hermeticum and the Latin Asclepius in a new English translation with notes and introduction*. Cambridge: Cambridge University Press.

—— (2015). *The Book of Magic: From Antiquity to the Enlightenment*. London: Random House.

Dhalla, Maneckji Nusservanji (1914). *Zoroastrian Theology: from the earliest times to the present day*. New York.

—— (1938). *History of Zoroastrianism*. Oxford: Oxford University Press.

Ford, Michael (2005). *Liber HVHI: Magick of the Adversary*. Lulu.

Kiesewetter, Karl (1987). *Der Occultismus des Altertums*. Hildesheim: Georg Olms. (Original work published 1896).

Kingsley, Peter (1990). The Greek Origin of the Sixth-Century Dating of Zoroaster. *Bulletin of the School of Oriental and African Studies* 53(2).

Moazami, Mahnaz (2005). Evil Animals in the Zoroastrian Religion. *History of Religions* 44 (4). University of Chicago Press.

Moore, George (1912). Zoroastrianism. *The Harvard Theological Review* 5(2).

Müller, Ernst (1997). *Der Sohar, Das heilige Buch der Kabbala*. Diederichs.

Müller, Friedrich Max (1899). *Theosophy Or Psychological Religion: the Gifford lectures delivered before the University of Glasgow in 1892*. Longmans, Green & Co.

Panati, Charles (1996). *Populäres Lexikon der religiösen Gegenstände und Gebräuche*. Eichborn.

Rätsch, Christian (2002). *Räucherstoffe: Der Atem des Drachen*. AT Verlag (First published 1996).

Reiner, Erica (1995). Astral Magic in Babylonia. *Transactions of the American Philosophical Society* 85(4), i–150.

Russell, J. R. (1993). On Mysticism and Esotericism among the Zoroastrians. *Iranian Studies* 26(1/2).

Scheftelowitz, Isidor (1920). *Die altpersische Religion und das Judentum*. Gießen.

Wake, William (Ed.) (1880). The Shepherd of Hermas. *The Apocryphal New Testament: being all the gospels, epistles, and other pieces now extant, attributed in the first four centuries to Jesus Christ, His apostles and their companions; and not included, by its compilers, in the authorized New Testament*. Philadelphia.

West, E. W. (1899). Notes on Zarathustra's Doctrine regarding the Soul. *Journal of the Royal Asiatic Society of Great Britain and Ireland*.

Westcott, William Wynn (1894). *The Divine Pymander of Hermes*. Collectanea Hermetica Vol.2. Golden Dawn Research Trust.

ANCIENT GREEK

Bremmer, Jan (1993). *The Early Greek Concept of the Soul*. Princeton: Princeton University Press. (First published 1987).

Burkert, Walter (1985). *Greek Religion*. Harvard: Harvard University Press.

Cherniss, Harold (1954). The Sources of Evil according to Plato. *Proceedings of the American Philosophical Society* 98(1), 23–30.

Chilcott, C. M. (1923). The Platonic Theory of Evil. *The Classical Quarterly* 17(1), 27–31.

Crowley, Aleister (2008). *Magick: Liber ABA, Book 4*, Parts I–IV. San Francisco: Weiser (First published 1913).

Greer, John Michael (2012). *The Blood of the Earth*. Dover: Scarlet Imprint.

Heinze, Richard (1892). *Xenocrates: Darstellung der Lehre und Sammlung der Fragmente*. Leipzig.

Hopfner, Theodor (1974). *Griechisch Ägyptischer Offenbarungszauber*, Band 1. Amsterdam.

—— (1983). *Griechisch Ägyptischer Offenbarungszauber*, Band 2. Amsterdam.

Luck, Georg (1986). *Arcana Mundi: Magic and the Occult in the Greek and Roman Worlds*. Johns Hopkins University Press.

Müller-Sternberg, Robert (1964). *Die Dämonen: Wesen und Wirkung eine Urphänomens*. Bremen: Carl Schünemann.

Agrippa, Heinrich Cornelius (1993). Edited and annotated by Donald Tyson. *Three Books of Occult Philosophy: A Complete Edition*. Llewellyn. (Originally published in 1651).

Pope, Alton (1969). *Daimonion of Socrates: a search for definition and an epistemological assessment*. Kansas State University.

Du Prel, Carl (1888). *Die Mystik der alten Griechen*. Leipzig: Ernst Günthers Verlag.

Rohde, Erwin (1898). *Seelenkult und Unsterblichkeitsglaube der Griechen*, Band I und II. Freiburg: Verlag Mohr.

Volquardsen, C. R. (1862). *Das Dämonium des Sokrates und seine Interpreten*. Kiel: Verlag von Karl Schröder.

Hanegraaff, Wouter J. (2006). *Dictionary of Gnosis & Western Esotericism*. Leiden: Brill.

PRACTICE

Bergman, Jan (1982). An Ancient Egyptian Theogony in a Greek Magical Papyrus (PGM VII, ll 516–521). *Studies in Egyptian Religion: Dedicated to Professor Jan Zandee*, edited by Heerma van Voss et al. Leiden: Brill.

Berlin, Adele (2011). *The Oxford Dictionary of the Jewish Religion* (2nd edition). Oxford University Press.

Betz, Hans Dieter (1981). The Delphic Maxim "Know Yourself" in the Greek Magical Papyri. *History of Religions* 21(2), 156–171. University of Chicago Press.

Böhme, Jakob. Sex Puncta Mystica. *Jakob Böhme's Sämmtliche Werke*, edited by K. W. Schiebler (1846). Leipzig: Sechster Band.

Buber, Martin (1908). *Die Legende des Baal-Shem*. Frankfurt am Main.

—— (1909). *Ekstatische Konfessionen*. Diederichs.

—— (1934). *Erzählungen von Engeln, Geistern und Dämonen*. Berlin.

—— (1955). *The Legend of the Baal-Shem*. Routledge.

—— (1966). *The Way of Man, According to the Teaching of the Hasidim*. Citadel Press.

Dehn, Georg (Ed.) (2001). *Buch Abramelin*. Edition Araki.

—— (2011). *The Book of Abramelin: A New Translation*. Nicolas-Hays.

Fauth, Wolfgang (1997). *Helios Megistos: Zur Synkretistischen Theologie der Spätantike*. Leiden: Brill.

Forrest, Adam P. (2016). *Liber Spiritum: A compendium of Writings on Angels & Other Spirits in Modern Magick*. Azoth Press.

Heiler, Friedrich (1920). *Das Gebet: Eine religionsgeschichtliche und religionspsychologische Untersuchung*. München.

Janzen, James D.(2015). *Psalms, Hymns and Spiritual Songs: The Road to Unity and Spiritual Maturity*. Friesen Press.

Jungkurth, Marcus M. Neither-Neither: Austin Osman Spare and the Underworld. https://fulgur.co.uk/austin-osman-spare/neither-neither-austin-osman-spare-underworld

Pachoumi, Eleni (2017). *The Concepts of the Divine in the Greek Magical Papyri*. Mohr Siebeck.

Selig, Gottfried (1972). *Sepher Schimmusch Tehillim, oder Gebrauch der Palme zum leiblichen Wohl der Menschen*. Berlin. (First published in 1788).

Scholem, Gershom (1977). *Von der mystischen Gestalt der Gottheit*. Suhrkamp.

Skinner, Stephen (2006). *The Complete Magician's Tables*. Golden Hoard Press.

Tyson, Donald (Ed.) (2009). *The Fourth Book of Occult Philosophy: The Companion to Three Books of Occult Philosophy*. Llewellyn.

Urban, Martina (2008). *Aesthetics of Revival: Martin Buber's Early Representation of the Hasidim as Kulturkritik*. University of Chicago Press.

INDEX

Made in the USA
Las Vegas, NV
11 December 2023